I Talk To Strangers

(here, there, and everywhere)

CAROLE CHANDLER

BALBOA.
PRESS

A DIVISION OF HAY HOUSE

Balboa Press books may be ordered through booksellers or by contacting:

Balboa Press
A Division of Hay House
1663 Liberty Drive
Bloomington, IN 47403
www.balboapress.com
1-(877) 407-4847

Because of the dynamic nature of the Internet, any web addresses or links contained in this book may have changed since publication and may no longer be valid. The views expressed in this work are solely those of the author and do not necessarily reflect the views of the publisher, and the publisher hereby disclaims any responsibility for them.

The author of this book does not dispense medical advice or prescribe the use of any technique as a form of treatment for physical, emotional, or medical problems without the advice of a physician, either directly or indirectly. The intent of the author is only to offer information of a general nature to help you in your quest for emotional and spiritual well-being. In the event you use any of the information in this book for yourself, which is your constitutional right, the author and the publisher assume no responsibility for your actions.

Any people depicted in stock imagery provided by Thinkstock are models, and such images are being used for illustrative purposes only.
Certain stock imagery © Thinkstock.

Printed in the United States of America

ISBN: 978-1-4525-6701-3 (sc)
ISBN: 978-1-4525-6703-7 (hc)
ISBN: 978-1-4525-6702-0 (e)

Library of Congress Control Number: 2013900887

Balboa Press rev. date: 1/18/2013

*

I talk to strangers. Why? They talk to me

Have strangers always talked to me? Not a chance

What changed? Me

Why did I change? Well something had to be done

How did I change? Focus

What was the result? Misery to joy in one lifetime

Can anyone create this change? Yes anyone

*

Changes took place in every aspect of my existence and I started experiencing a profound difference in the way people responded to me, everywhere I went.

Over time I told a few friends about what someone said here or what another person said there. They enjoyed my tales and suggested I share my experiences. I considered writing a book but hesitated about where, when and how.

Then I went to Ireland for a few days this year and the result was my first book.

This is my second. Enjoy.

*

It was a bumper day for talking to strangers, just like the day before and the day before that and the day before that. It seems that every day is special, every day is a new adventure, every day is fun. I live in a busy vibrant area of south west London and have learned to accept that talking to strangers is something that I do. I have no need to encourage the conversations and I continue to be amused by people's willingness to chat. Sit back, relax and join me in a few memories of when I talked to strangers and they talked to me.

I feel like beginning with an encounter about a lady that I met at a bus stop in London. I noticed her beforehand as I was walking along the road. Way ahead of me, way down the road, her hair caught my attention. Swaying with a life of its own, her golden, shoulder length, straight hair moved like a piece of satin floating in the breeze. I was a long way behind and as I enjoyed watching her hair, I remembered a couple of times when I have seen beautiful hair in the street and followed the urge to express my delight to the owner. Thankfully, they have never seemed to mind and I am always grateful for it because it is not nearly so much fun paying compliments that are not well received. It is like offering a gift and having it rejected.

Anyway, the wafting satin crossed the road ahead of me and disappeared out of view, so I turned my attention to something else. When I arrived at the bus stop, there was the hair again. Now she was standing next to me and

I felt the urge to say something. I knew that I did not have to. I could have just as easily kept my thoughts to myself. The urge got the better of me, as I concluded that I may never see her again and there was nothing to lose.

Standing beside her I said, "Excuse me." She continued to look ahead, no response, no response at all. I tried again, "Excuse me." With the second attempt, she glanced towards me, smiled, flicked her hair back and removed her earphones.

"Oh sorry, I didn't hear you with my earphones in, were you talking to me?"

Well that explained her previous lack of response. I was overjoyed to see that she was happy to stop her listening and interact with me.

"I'm sorry to interrupt you but I just wanted to say that I noticed your beautiful hair from way down the road."

"Oh really, thank you. I've just straightened it otherwise it looks terrible."

"Surely not, well it looks gorgeous today. It really caught my attention as it floated from side to side when you walked." She thanked me again so I continued,

"It looks like satin swaying in the breeze and even on a cloudy day like today, with no sun, your hair was shining."

"Oh, it's so kind of you to say that, you're so sweet."

"I'm just inspired to say what I feel."

I had said all I wanted to say and expected her to return to her listening but no. She continued by telling me how she washes and straightens her hair daily, even though it is quite a commitment but she feels it is necessary because she prefers that way. I gently offered the option of leaving it natural and she agreed that if she did, she would probably get used to it. On occasions when she has previously grown tired of the morning routine, she tried to get used to the curls and the frizz but never felt entirely happy.

The stop is served by two routes and without knowing where I was going, she told me that we had just missed one but she did not know about the other. I told her that I had walked from about four stops away and had not seen one, so felt confident that it would arrive soon. This of course added to my amusement because I could have easily waited for a bus at any of the earlier stops, thus saving myself the walk, or indeed I might have walked all the way which is what I usually do. Either way I would have missed out on the fun of our conversation.

By that point I guessed our chat was at an end and once again I fully expected her to return to her earphones. I was wrong.

"I'm all out of breath because I've got a deviated septum and it makes it hard for me to breathe. I'm due to have an operation so hopefully I won't get so breathless." Though unexpected, it was nice of her to share this information with me. Her nose looked perfect, she did not look like an amateur or professional boxer, or indeed someone who might have been involved in a pub brawl, so with vague interest I asked,

"How come it's a problem now, hasn't it always been like it?"

"No, not really, I've had two operations but it's not brilliant. The hospital has agreed to do it again but can't guarantee it will be successful. It's really a problem when I walk quickly and I like walking because it feels so good."

I agreed with her that walking is great exercise and suggested that she might perhaps try walking slower but she said that then it feels like she is not really doing anything. When I said that walking is beneficial at any speed, she laughed and pointed out that had she been walking slower that morning, then her hair would not have moved the same way. I followed up with the realisation that her hair would have indeed looked different, then a random stranger would not have stopped to talk to her at the bus stop and we would not have been enjoying our conversation.

She added that she also had breathing difficulties because she was just getting over a cold. With that she stepped back and said,

"Don't worry, I won't give it to you."

In turn, I told her not to worry because I would not catch it anyway. I used to catch colds all the time but not anymore.

"Oh you're lucky."

"It's not luck. I have changed my life to make it so."

"What did you do? Was it food, did you start eating the right foods?"

I told her that I have always eaten pretty well, so do not really concentrate on it. When she asked again, I confessed that the main thing I did was reduce my stress.

"Really? Was that what you did?"

"Well yes, stress reduces your ability to fight off infections, it leaves you open to catching things."

When she said that she thought I might be right, I felt inclined to say not 'might' but decided to let it go. I shared with her that I used to have regular chest infections a few times a year. They were of great severity reducing my ability to function and live my life comfortably. This was my normal until a few years ago. Now not even a sniffle.

She said, "I suppose people do have stress but I don't have any, I don't worry about money, I'm fine."

Interesting that she chose to say that, who mentioned money? I have learned to take little notice of people who claim to be free of stress when their physical expression indicates otherwise. I remember a client who was emotional and seemingly close to tears, insisting he had no stress in his life and volunteered to tell me that his mother had recently died and he was daily visiting his best friend who was terminally ill in hospital. No stress? Really?

The bus stop lady continued, "Sometimes I think I might not have enough to pay a bill or a credit card, or I might be concerned about paying off my loan, or not have enough to pay my rent or something like that."

"You said you don't worry about money but those are all financial concerns."

She continued, "And I'm unemployed at the moment so that doesn't help."

"That's another stressor."

"Oh, I've just been diagnosed with arthritis, so that doesn't help."

"That's another stressor."

"Then there's my hair. I have to get up really early to straighten it every day."

"That's another stressor."

Woah! Not a bad list for someone with no stress. No wonder she had a cold. She thought that perhaps I was right to mention the link and had remembered reading something about that somewhere. She had given me a lot of information in a short space of time. I should not have been surprised, I have experienced this before. I offered my perspective that she seemed to be experiencing a lot to occupy her attention and perhaps stress was a contributory factor to her 'catching' a cold. I pointed out that thoughts about her bills, such as if and how they will be paid, is worrying about money. She reflected and agreed. I felt no need to say any more. I felt no need to hear any more. She had made the connection herself.

It may seem that we were stranded at this bus stop for hours but really no, we were there just a few minutes. The bus came. As I boarded, the handsome smiling face of the driver was a momentary distraction.

As lively and as lovely as it was, I had no expectation of continuing my conversation with the silken haired lady on the bus. The bus was busy, I chose a place to stand, and she chose to stand beside me. I did not expect her to, it was nice that she did but I did not mind either way. We talked about hair again, her hair, my hair, her friend's hair, the cost of hairdressers and the frequency of treatments. We talked and laughed. Our journey was most entertaining. I enjoyed her company and she clearly enjoyed mine as when we arrived at her stop, she was sad to leave. How lovely to share a fond farewell with an acquaintance of such short duration. Life is sweet.

*

There is something about travelling by bus that seems to lend itself so well to meeting people. I have a plethora of experiences involving this mode of transport. So many that I have decided to devote them to a separate book. For now, I shall continue with non-bus related tales, except for the one or two which might creep in here because I cannot wait to share them.

I hopped off the bus which conveniently stops right beside the post office and is just a few doors away from where I see my clients for energy balancing treatments. It was like so many post offices at lunchtime, busy. I had no idea of the exact time, I rarely do. I was due at work but had given myself plenty of time from leaving home, so felt no concerns about joining the queue for the post office counter at the back of the shop.

I happily looked around with the intention of finding something to feel good about, something to keep me 'in the moment', something on which to focus my thoughts, something to appreciate. I heard a voice behind me,

"One, two, three, four, five, six." I turned and saw a sweet little lady standing behind me. I tried to ignore her evident appearance of agitation, as she turned towards the front of the shop and began again, "One, two, three, four, five, six." She looked back and me, I smiled, she told me she was counting the number of people in each queue and trying to decide which might be quicker. She even stood on the bottom shelf beside us to get a better view over our heads.

Carole Chandler

Well, I could have sympathised because I used to do exactly what she was doing. You know how it is, when trying to minimise waiting time by counting queues in post offices and supermarkets. It is usually a fruitless activity. How many times have we chosen the shorter queue, only to be thwarted by an unexpected interruption like customer queries, price checks or management intervention? Thankfully, the whole queue mentality has changed for me since learning the value of changing my perspective. Now I just stand somewhere, expect all to be well, know that all will be well and understand that we will all be attended to in good time.

So there I was with this delightful lady who was clearly not altogether comfortable with her place in the shop. She openly considered her options, I listened. She wondered whether the six people before her, might move quicker than the six people in the other queue, by the counter at the front of the shop. She asked me what I thought. I resisted the temptation to say that I did not mind either way and simply said that I thought she was in the right place exactly where she was.

I was happy with my response. I felt comfortable with my way of thinking. I suspect that my words were not what she wanted to hear. She looked at me quizzically and asked if I knew of any other post offices locally. Well, now she was just being daft. I mean the whole two queues debate was bad enough but to consider going somewhere else could hardly be a sensible option. It may have been a good move if she could relocate herself with a happy heart and a content disposition but from her place of worry and frustration she would be unlikely to find herself in an improved situation.

I told her where the nearest alternative office was but gently pointed out that it may well have a queue of its own of equal length or longer, not to mention the time it would take to walk to the other side of town. Feeling calm, I looked at her and with a smile said,

"You're fine here, we'll be served soon enough."

She attempted to open a discussion about the demise of the nation's post offices, the closure of facilities, the follies of the government and sadness of job losses. I did not feel inclined to join her, partly because I do not agree and partly because I am not bothered enough about how many there are around the country. The one I was in at that moment was just fine.

The queue moved a little. We found ourselves standing by shelves of greeting cards with beautiful photographs of baby animals. My companion continued to fragment her attention so I said,

"Look, the queue is moving, let's just enjoy the photos of the cute animals, look at the kittens and puppies." The cards were working for me, the animals were so cute and the quality of photography seemed too good for greetings cards, from what I could see at first glance. She looked at the selection and grunted,

"Do you like cats?" My response was easy,

"What's not to like, they are so cute." She said she preferred dogs, so I added, "Okay, there are puppies, foxes and penguins." Mentioning the penguins seemed to be a winner and distracted her for long enough for her to agree, that the one in the picture was cute. Then she said,

"They smell though, I saw some in South Africa." Ouch! For a moment there we were so close. She released her negative thoughts for an instant to acknowledge the cuteness of the baby penguin but for some reason chose to focus her attention on the smell, when we were looking at photographs, which had no smell included. Oh well, I guess it was up to her. Anyway, I told her that I was not aware that penguins lived in South Africa. I had visited a colony in Argentina many years ago and indeed they did smell but you do not get a sense of that when you see them on television or at the movies.

She had not seen 'Happy Feet' which was a pity because I am a huge fan and we could have talked about Mumble, Gloria, Eric, Ramone and his amigos for long enough to keep our mind off our waiting time. We chatted briefly about the astonishing filmography of 'March of the Penguins' then she started flitting her attention around the shop again.

Now then, of course I did not have to bother with her. Of course I could have simply ignored her. Of course I could have maintained my own focus and left her to her own distractions. Perhaps she was happy being anxious. Perhaps she was content in her agitation. I know that her inner workings of her mind are none of my business. Yet she chose to include me,

"Oh this is taking a long time, I might go over there." Again she asked me whether I thought that she should move. At the risk of repeating myself I said,

"The queue is moving, we will be served soon, just look at the cute animals, just enjoy them for the moment." There was that quizzical look again.

"I'm thinking about what I have to do back at work."

"What? While you're here, why do that to yourself? Put your attention back on the cute animals."

She tilted her head while looking at me and said, "You're very focused are you?"

My response was easy, "I have to be." I considered adding 'if I am to be joyful' but I decided against it. Well, for that moment anyway.

She said, "It must be genetic." Well over the years I have learned to ignore people's perceptions and misinterpretations of me but I was not in the frame of mind to let that one go, oh no.

"It is definitely not genetic. I have changed my life in many ways and made the conscious decision to focus."

"You did it consciously?"

"Yes, oh yes. If my genes had anything to do with it, I would not be here now and we would certainly not be having this conversation." She continued with the subject of genetics and said a few things about parenting, how they were from a different age group (of course) and how they held a different philosophy for life. She was in danger of dragging herself down a different, not so happy path again, so I said,

"They did their best, let it go."

She looked at me, paused, and smiled, "You're so calm".

I replied, "It's what I do."

Time had moved on. We were at the front and next to be served, so before we parted company I said,

"There you are, bet you're glad you didn't run off now, we're at the front of the queue already."

It was another interesting interaction, one which I will never know the effects of but I have no doubt that I have learned something from her.

*

Both of those meetings were on the same day before I even started work, they were lengthy interactions with strangers, giving me the opportunity to remind myself and demonstrate to them that my outlook on life is neither the result of luck nor genetics.

The next day brought another set of encounters. One was with a sweet young lady who was growing her first baby which was due to be born in three weeks. She looked well and said that she felt well, was experiencing a comfortable pregnancy and 'making the most of' her last couple of weeks of 'freedom'. I thought it was an interesting perspective. She had listened to many well-meaning people who had apparently told her to expect her life to change for the worse after the arrival of her baby. Interesting. I offered the suggestion that the baby's arrival may prove to be a joyous occasion, one to bring happiness and fulfilment to her family life. She considered it as a new view and thanked me for giving her an alternative option. It was my pleasure.

Later, I was chatting happily to our receptionist when another member of staff called me to speak a lady who had come in looking for me. I was pleased to hear that she had come especially to receive one of my sample hand massages. I was happy partly because I so enjoy giving them and partly because I am full of joy for the person receiving them. Over time I have come to understand the great benefit that is received on so many levels. I offer a selection of lotions, creams and oils from which they can choose. Often people ask me, which I think is the best, I say the same thing to everyone, that they are all good for the massage, which is why I am happy to use them. The question of choice is personal and I leave it entirely to them. On the occasions when a client feels unable to make their own choice (and there can be several reasons for that) I will then use my guidance to make the decision. They always agree, it makes me chuckle to myself sometimes.

I set up a table on the shop floor surrounded by shelves of products so, often we have shoppers browsing, choosing, talking to a companion or talking on the phone, while my client sits in front of me, eyes closed, relaxing. Also, my position in the shop is beside the entrance, which leads out to the main road and is right beside a major junction of constant traffic and a family of traffic lights. There is music playing in the shop, there are people talking in the shop, there is enough to distract most people inside and outside. I continue to offer my hand massages there because they work. It is possible to relax even in that environment. For me it is about focus. This is what I know and I am sharing what I know.

If there is noise, I just continue. I never apologise, after all it is not anyone's fault is it? So apology is not required. I have learned to focus my own attention whatever the circumstances (well at least I try) so that is a skill I feel I am sharing with my client, even during a ten minute hand massage. It is all good.

Anyway, there I was chatting to our wonderful new receptionist, well she is not so new now and she happily lets me rattle on about spirituality. The lady asked,

"Do you remember me?" When I am asked that question, I would sincerely love to be able to employ my memory and give her date, time, place and circumstance, along with a detailed transcription of our conversation, perhaps including her attire of the moment. However, that was hardly likely to happen. I have had a client in my room for an hour, giving them my hundred per cent attention during a treatment, allowing energy to flow through me for their benefit and relief, then the next day I have not recognised their face let alone remembered their name.

This aspect of the new me, bothered me for a while. I had to clear up my feelings around the discrepancy between loving the person while apparently not remembering them. Luckily, no one seems to mind. Some say that it is an indication of cerebral impairment but I have had it explained to me, that it is just a filtering of information, an indication of my living in the moment, of being present, of maintaining my focus and attention in my current time and space. Thankfully, there are contrasting moments where I may remember names and faces of people from perhaps the briefest of interactions. It is all good.

This lovely lady helped me out by reminding me of a brief visit she had made in the shop, several weeks before, when she was with her son, who had held my attention while he engaged with me from his buggy. Well yes, children will do that. She returned alone to treat herself to a hand massage, from me on the shop floor. I was pleased to hear it and I was happy to oblige.

After choosing her lotion she settled, closed her eyes ready to receive. At the end, she sat for a couple of minutes with her eyes still closed, while I congratulated myself on a job well done. I felt my inner peace in my meditative state, which is a feeling I always enjoy after giving a massage. Her eyes opened briefly then closed, then flickered, reluctant to stay open. I was not bothered. I was in no hurry. She did not want to leave, she was enjoying the moment. I told her that she was fine, that we were open for another five hours, so I had no intention of rushing her. However, she had a son to collect from nursery so was not in a position to consider the stay-in-the-chair-all-afternoon option, no matter how much she would have liked to accept. She looked at me and smiled saying,

"It's amazing how you really can block everything out." I agreed. She continued, "Even with the noise outside, it's possible to block it out." She was right and I was glad that she had made this discovery. I was glad for her. Glad that she had realised she had the power, particularly considering that a police car with sirens blazing had paused right outside and a motorbike engine sang its tune while revving at the lights. I congratulated her and said that understanding our ability to block things out is a huge step in personal development. It can be done and is worth striving for. She said that it felt good knowing that and suggested that it would be worth practising. I told her that she was describing my life, my way of living, this is what I do.

It was a wonderful interaction, she was happy and I was happy. As with everyone I meet, I allowed myself to be me and I learned something from her. Meeting her reminded me of my ability to focus and I was happy that she was able to take something away with her.

*

Later the same day I had packed away my table from the shop floor and had just returned upstairs for the basket of towels and paper when I passed a lady standing near the top of the stairs. She looked at me, smiled and waited. I meet so many people and this lady looked familiar. I asked,

"Where do I recognise you from?"

"Here, I've shopped here and once you gave me excellent clear directions to Tooting but I didn't follow them."

Well as soon as she said that, I immediately remembered the lively conversation with her the previous week. I had been sitting at my table upstairs when she stood nearby talking to another member of staff. She had apparently expressed an interest in finding a good curry house and one of our lads was recommending a restaurant in our lovely vibrant south west London area of Tooting. They discussed how to get there by bus then the chap said,

"Let's ask Carole, she'll know how to get there by bus, she knows the bus routes." Well I could not argue with that, as I am a fond traveller of our London bus network and they were chatting about my area. They brought me up to speed with their conversation and asked for my input,

"Of course," I said, "the 57, 131, 219 and the 493 all go to Tooting from here, where exactly do you need to get to?"

After confirming she needed to be on the high street after the Broadway, before Tooting Bec, I continued, "Then the easiest way for you is to catch the 219 from around the corner here. It begins in Wimbledon and the first stop is opposite Sainsbury's. Turn right out of the door, turn right at the traffic lights, it's just a minute away."

We worked out that she needed to get off at the stop after Tooting Broadway. I was confident that she would be fine, it would be an easy journey and easy to know where to get off. I was far less concerned about how she would manage on the bus than how she might cope in Tooting High Street. With no judgement intended, I observed that she was a small, quiet lady, well dressed, softly spoken, who might look more comfortable heading towards Wimbledon Village rather than Tooting Bec. I know the area, I adore the diversity, I know how to keep my wits about me and am accustomed to the variety of personalities frequently encountered. I also understand the speed of pedestrian traffic in this familiar part of town. I tried not to be concerned for her but asked if she was ready for such a vibrant shopping area. She said,

"Oh, I'm looking forward to it, I want to go somewhere lively." Well good for her. With our good wishes we hoped she would enjoy her meal and off she went.

So that was the previous week and here she was telling me that she had not followed my instructions.

"Oh dear, did you get lost?" I already could not imagine how because she had just said that my directions were clear. What could have possibly gone wrong?

"I ended up in Kingston." Now, she must have been having a laugh. How was that even possible?

"How? The 219 doesn't even go to Kingston. You must have caught a different bus." She told me how but she could not tell me why she had for some reason caught the 57 from outside Sainsbury's instead of the 219 from opposite Sainsbury's. She was on the wrong side of the road, so not only a different bus number but she went in a different direction. The 57 going the correct way, would have at least got her to Tooting. That would have been more understandable because it turns right at the Broadway, so she might have later got lost somewhere in the area. Oh dear, to find herself heading towards Kingston, was way off course, poor lady.

She felt bad enough already so I decided not to dwell on it and said,

"Next time you'll have an easier journey and you will get there just fine."

So, I asked her what she thought about the vibrancy of Tooting? She sighed. As it had taken her so long to get there, she was really hungry and really tired, so did not stay very long. She felt that there were people everywhere. Well that is a common impression of London streets. She complained that she felt them pushing and it was hard for her to walk anywhere. It felt so crowded for her, that she moved to the side of the pavement and retreated into shop doorways to wait for people to walk by. She found it too busy and uncomfortable.

I did listen to her perspective, I was happy to listen, I am usually happy to listen. I said that many people say the same thing, especially about walking around our capital city. She seemed pleased to hear that and replied that it was good to know that others felt the same. She asked me how they cope and I said,

"They don't go to places in London, they move out to the country to avoid the crowds." She said she understood.

For some reason I felt inspired to tell her that my experience is quite different. Often when I have a free day, I will go to central London just for the fun of walking around simply because I love the buzz. I cannot say that I notice the crowds. I do not notice groups of pushing people. On the contrary, I see groups of people walking towards me and they seem to part, for me to pass by. It seems like I do not have to do anything and a space appears. She listened with interest.

She asked, "What do you think makes the difference?"

My instinctive response was to say, "How I feel about myself."

She pondered and replied, "Sometimes I think my boundary for personal space is further out than most people." Well that was like an 'ah ha' moment, a light bulb moment, an epiphany, call it what you like, I just wanted to say BINGO!

Her insight inspired me to say, "That's a good point well made." Stretching my arms out wide in front of her right there in the shop, I continued with, "I'm feel like this, open arms, come on in."

It was interesting for me because her comment really helped me to realise quite how much I have changed. She mentioned that her personal space extends a long way. I understood this, I was there once. I was there for a long time. Not only was my boundary extreme, it was a force field. Anyway, that was then and this is now. Now I am ready to embrace me as I am. Now I am ready to embrace others as they choose to be. I have no need to protect myself from anyone or anything, so my personal boundary is in a place of comfort and I am happy just to be me. Like I said previously, I feel like I am open hearted with arms extended, so come on in.

This may be an appropriate place to mention my hugging history which I wrote about in some detail in my book 'I Talk to Strangers – to be sure, to be sure, to be sure' which was joyfully inspired by my holiday to Ireland.

Those hugging experiences had a significant impact on my journey to my current emotional place. Interestingly, the same day I had the Tooting journey conversation with this lovely lady, a work colleague told me something that she had said to a prospective client who asked about my reiki work. "Carole has this aura of calm and peace, she is in a bubble, a bright clear bubble with the pollution outside."

I was touched by her words, then she amazed me by adding, "Nothing bothers her, she lets you into her bubble and that's why you feel so good when you are with her."

Well, I nearly cried when I heard her words, I felt quite emotional. So much for nothing bothering me, her words did affect me, in a nice positive way of course. I told her that I was touched and she said, "That is how I see you." I would never have known. I could not possibly have known. I was unaware that anyone saw me like that. I was touched indeed. Her words reminded me of something a wise person once said, *'we never touch anyone so lightly that we do not leave a mark'.*

All of this said I decided to congratulate myself on my achievements. Anyone can do this. Anyone can change the way they feel about themself. Anyone can change the way others feel about them. It is simple but not necessarily easy. It takes effort. It takes focus. Whether it is worth it or not, is a choice for each individual.

I chatted a little longer with the sweet lady in the shop, felt a desire to move on, gave her a hug, wished her well and we parted.

*

So, not bad for two days of interactions with people I did not know. These are fairly indicative of a day in the life of ... well, me. Now each day is fun, now each day is an adventure. I wake up in the morning with gleeful anticipation wondering who will be sent to play with me, to meet me, to talk to me, to smile with me and to interact with me today. My stories are even more fun because so many of them happen in our busy capital where we are told the people are unfriendly and uncaring. My experience is quite different so this is another reason that I am inspired to share.

During the last few years, I have entertained friends and family with my daily encounters and have been encouraged to share them, to write them down, to publish them. Well this is all well and good but I had no idea how to begin. I had never written a book before. Surely you have to be trained in that sort of thing. Then I went on holiday to Ireland for a week a few months ago and my first book wrote itself. I could hardly believe it. I began writing on my first day away and made copious notes of my continuous observations and meetings.

The writing bug had well and truly bitten. I went to sleep thinking about my book, I woke up thinking about my book, I had vivid dreams about my book. I lived, breathed and tasted my book. What a powerful creative force this whole writing business has turned out to be. I thought my meditation inspired art was gripping enough because I have grown accustomed to waking at five in the morning with the urge to paint, given in to the urge for an hour or so, then gone back to sleep.

A couple of years ago I began carrying a pretty little book with me. It is a cute hard backed note book covered in red fabric with Chinese patterns. I bought it in a lovely shop in London's Covent Garden, felt inspired to carry it everywhere and soon it was full of notes about the people and conversations which I had on a daily basis. It seemed that every bus journey, visit to a shop, meal in a restaurant or walk down a road offered an opportunity for note taking. I am so glad I felt inspired to do all of this. Now this book can take shape. I began with strangers I met one day after the other. I have not really decided how to proceed, however as I mentioned before, the bus tales will be devoted to a publication of their own, unless I have a particularly strong desire to include it here.

Let us see how I get on, I have a sneaking suspicion that once I get going, it will unfold.

*

People seem to just come up to me for all sorts of reasons. There was the time when I was in a supermarket on the Northcote Road in Clapham Junction, or some might say Battersea depending on who is speaking I think. Well, I do not live there so it does not matter much to me. Anyway, I was looking for toothpaste and to all in intents and purposes I assumed that I looked like a regular shopper. Carrying my basket with a few items, I wore my coat, scarf and gloves when a woman passed behind me, came closer, stood beside me and without introduction said,

"I am having trouble with my digestion. I'm not going to the toilet properly, can you recommend something, what shall I do?" Admittedly, she is free to talk to anyone she wishes but there she was selecting me for specific medical advice. It begged the question, why me? Why me indeed? I looked at her, wondering vaguely if we had met before. There was probably no real point me wasting my time or energy wondering why she asked me, I shall leave that to other people.

It transpired that she had been suffering from constipation for about a week and wondered whether there was something she could buy in the supermarket or whether she should go to the doctor instead. I offered a suggestion. She listened. She had not thought of increasing her fruit and veg intake, or drinking more water than normal. She seemed happy to try this first, thanked me and disappeared. Interesting.

*

Then there was the Saturday afternoon when I found myself waiting by the traffic lights of a busy crossroads also on the same Northcote Road as it happens. It was a sunny day and there were many people about. Anyone who knows this pretty area of London will be aware of the plethora of bars, pubs, cafes and restaurants. There is such an abundance of places to eat and drink that I often wonder how there can be enough business to sustain them all. I suppose I do not need to worry really, especially considering how they are sometimes full on the inside, with hoards of customers spilling out across the pavement.

Anyway, it was a busy Saturday afternoon and I waited at the pedestrian crossing in a crowd of about fifteen people. I noticed a young lady walk towards us and thought nothing of it except perhaps to assume that she too wished to cross the road when the lights changed. I was wrong. She walked through the bunch of people, passing in front of one, then another, then another and stood in front of me with her back to the road. I was feeling good, I had no concerns and I smiled at her.

She said, "Excuse me, can you tell me the way to Waitrose, is it this way or that way?" I knew the area and I knew the way, so I was happy to direct her. She smiled, thanked me, passed people on her way out of the waiting huddle and disappeared. Interesting. Why me? Why me indeed?

*

Then there was the time I was in TKMaxx in Hammersmith, I am a fan of this chain of stores but had never been in that branch before and was pleased to discover a lovely coat. I was admiring the beauty of it on the hanger when a woman spoke to me from the other side of the rail,

"You look like someone who has happy thoughts in her mind." Well I was impressed by her observation and could not argue with it. I told her that I always try to have happy thoughts and had found a gorgeous coat. She came round to my side and she did not seem the slightest bit interested in what I was looking at. This was just as well because I had already decided that I really liked it and did not want to have to fight her for it. She kept watching me and I continued to drool over my coat. I tried it on while she seemed happy to just stand there. I found a mirror and entertained myself while I paraded in front of it and she followed me. I did not mind her attention, I was having fun and she was not bothering me, so as she was still there I said,

"I love this huge hood, the angle of the sleeves and this cute hem. It's a quirky coat but I think I can pull it off."

She told me I looked great and I had to agree. I finished swanning around, told her I was definitely going to treat myself, said good bye and wandered over to the other side of the store. A couple of minutes later she reappeared, told me that she had really enjoyed chatting to me and admired my joyful spirit. She asked me what I do for a living and when I told her, I thought it

29

was really sweet of her to say that I am a good advertisement for my work. I happily gave her my number when she asked for it and had no problem with her idea of meeting for coffee some time. She seemed nice enough so where could be the harm in that? My daughter had an entirely different view and told me her opinion of the proceedings with great merriment. It is wonderful having teenagers to offer an alternative perspective of events.

*

Clothes are a great conversation starter and a super way to meet people. I was in a fancy restaurant in Covent Garden when I saw a handsome couple arrive. I imagine that everyone saw them, they were spectacular. Each of them tall, slim and fashionably well-dressed, then I caught sight of her shoes. It would have been next to impossible to miss those babies. Her red satin peep toed court shoe, with ridiculously high heels were just crying out to be admired, so I made it my job to talk to her about them on the way out.

I briefly apologised to the chap for interrupting their evening, as they sat in an alcove, probably trying to enjoy a romantic night out. Well, lucky me, I was glad to find that the lovely girl was more than a little bit pleased by my interest in her foot wear. She was quite delightful and appeared to be genuinely happy that I had asked about them and called me sweet for talking to her. She seemed content enough to tell me that it was the first time she had worn them, they had cost a fortune, they were killing her feet but we somehow agreed that the sheer beauty of them was worth the financial and physical pain. I say somehow agreed because I have never been keen on putting appearance before comfort but then again I was not turning heads by wearing what she was wearing, so I commend her.

Then there was the impeccably well-dressed lady who walked slowly and tentatively down the steps in Covent Garden's Marks and Spencers. She paused and stepped aside when she saw me coming and I was immediately distracted by her divine shoes. The black patent open toed creations with a high (very high) gold coloured thin elegant heel, seemed to be the reason for her slow progress down the steps. I did not have to say anything but I was feeling playful. She looked at me when I overtook her, so I smiled and said,

"Your shoes are more beautiful than mine but I'm faster than you." She laughed and told me that they had cost a fortune, were really uncomfortable and she wished she had not bought them. Once again I found myself saying that they were beautiful so it was worth it. Yes they were beautiful but I am not so sure about the worth it part. I am not one to wear uncomfortable shoes but I do like to see beauty and that includes beautiful footwear.

Then there was the time I enjoyed lunch with a dear friend of mine in Streatham when I interrupted our conversation because I spotted a woman at the counter wearing a pair of Doc Martin boots. So what is so special about that? Nothing really, we see plain black DMs every day of the week but these had something red on the side and I could not quite see what it was. That was not good enough for me, I had to have a closer look, so as she passed our table on her way out, I put my hand on her arm and said hallo. She beamed a lovely, friendly, bright smile at me, like she knew me, which I thought was wonderful. I asked for a closer look at her black boots to find out what the red was all about. They were flowers, not just flowers but roses. Well that was cute enough but wait for it, the flowers were embroidered.

Well I could hardly contain myself. This lovely lady clearly had a soft side and the contrast of her heavy boots (unlaced I might add) with embroidered flowers on the side, just made my day. She said that she does not see herself as girly but the flowers were her concession to femininity and I think she pulled it off really well. She said something about having to wear boots because of something to do with her feet and I pointed out that, if she were not wearing them, then I would not have stopped her and we would not have enjoyed our friendly chat. She was great.

Then there was the time I had selected some clothes to try on in a lovely shop in Chelsea when I heard someone offer to help me. I looked up and I mean up, to see a mass of black wavy hair surrounding the beautiful face of a tall, very tall, slim, very slim, goddess in an exquisite red dress. Her long, very long legs showing off her black patent high, very high heeled shoes. She was stunning and I could not help myself,

"Oh my goodness, look at you! What are you doing here, shouldn't you be on a cat-walk somewhere?"

She was truly gorgeous and she knew it, she loved my remark, laughed and called her colleague over to ask if she had heard what I had said. She then made me laugh when she told me that she was just working there temporarily. Perhaps until her next modelling assignment, I wondered. She said that was a dream but I suspect that it may soon be a reality.

*

I have stopped people inside and outside shops, I do not mind either way, just following my guidance. There was the time I overheard a conversation in Boots the chemists, in Covent Garden. A girl, about my daughter's age, was telling someone about her tiredness, her need to go to bed, her desire to catch up on much needed sleep. We left the shop at the same time and for some inexplicable reason I followed the urge to ask her about her sleep deprivation, wondering if it was the result of too many heavy nights out. No, I do not know why I did it, perhaps just sheer nosiness, perhaps a desire to be of assistance, who knows?

The suggestion of tiredness from partying made her laugh as she told me she wished that were the reason. Sadly, it was the consequence of university dissertation deadlines, nightly typing, pressure and stress, stress, stress. The more she spoke the more she let off steam. She did not seem to mind my question and told me about her hard work, determination, family interference and relationship concerns.

This lovely girl was getting herself into a bit of a state, so I made the executive decision to take control. She seemed willing, so I offered her a suggestion. I stopped her from talking. I asked her to close her eyes. There we were, outside on the pathway, with hundreds of people walking by, she trusted me enough to close her eyes and following my words, she took three deep breaths in, followed by three long slow exhalations.

My work was done. She opened her eyes and there before me was a different person. From her new place of greatly reduced agitation, she thanked me. I thanked her for trusting me. I was happy to leave her with this new skill which she could use any time she felt the need.

This was not a one off, as there was also the time I observed a young chap serving in a restaurant in Chelsea. His repeated apologies to the previous customer, his self-admonishment, repeated sighs and furrowed brow led me to look at him sympathetically and say, that he looked preoccupied. He sighed again telling me that he was going through a lot of problems and with no encouragement from me went on to tell me that his degree work, search for a job and moving home were all on his mind.

It was lunchtime and there were plenty of people milling about but I did not allow that to prevent me from giving this poor young chap my full attention. I asked him to close his eyes. Surprisingly he did. I was a little surprised because he was behind the counter and could have easily given me many reasons not to follow my suggestion or could have simply taken no notice of me. However, he closed them and I led him through three deep breaths. While we took this moment together, one of his colleagues stood beside him, she looked at him, looked at me and looked back at him but interestingly said nothing. When he reopened his eyes I said,

"Now, do you feel at least a teeny bit better?"

"Oh yes, I do feel much better, my head feels lighter, I have more energy, more oxygen has gone to my head."

My work was done.

Breathing is so powerful. Of course I know that we breathe automatically but focused breathing brings additional benefits beyond the basic physiological gaseous exchange of oxygen and carbon dioxide. I introduced this simple technique to a client, a performing arts student, who visited me for massage treatments, in an effort to reduce her pre-audition and performance anxiety. She was accustomed to breathing exercises taught by her college but she felt that the three breaths led by me were far more effective. I was honoured.

I lead all of my clients in a few deep breaths before every treatment, I believe in the power of our focus, I believe in the power of our breath, combine the two and bingo. Yes, bingo, we have meditation. It really is that simple. Meditation can be the mystery that some people make it or it can simply be focused breathing. Just focus and breathe, breathe and focus then experience the world change.

*

So, now it is time to return to random conversations with random people. There was the night that I was out dancing at a jive venue with some friends and as always a lot of strangers. I found myself sitting beside a lady who I had never met before. She began by telling me that she had enjoyed watching me and delighted me by saying lots of complimentary gorgeous things about my dancing. What a sweetie she was. I am never going to complain about strangers who are willing to pay compliments. It is always wonderful to be appreciated.

I have no idea how it happened but during the next few minutes she told me details about her health, her sister's health, her mother's health and her concerns about all three. A pal of mine returned to invite me to dance and this lady said to him,

"I don't know this lady and I'm telling her all of these things about my family and I don't even know why." Then she looked at me and said, "I'm sorry, I have no idea why I'm telling you all this."

My pal said, "Don't worry, it's okay, she has that effect on people."

I got up to enjoy a wonderful dance with him and never saw her again.

*

This scenario of people telling me personal stuff appears to be a common theme with me and has been over the years. When I look back I realise that I used to encourage it. I was not even aware of it at the time, I just thought it happened because I was a nurse, however, I have come to understand that while my medical knowledge, background and experience may have been a contributory factor, there was more to it than that.

I think that I encouraged people to share their troubles, which was easy because people love to spill out details and give graphic information. Of course while they were talking about their personal stuff, I could avoid talking about mine. It took me a long time to realise that people rarely asked. I had developed a wonderful knack of attracting people who had little interest in me. They drained me of my energy as they took and took and took from me and gave nothing back. Thankfully, this has all changed. I know how the world works now so I no longer blame them and I no longer blame myself. Everyone is free to be exactly as they choose to be.

*

There have been occasions when people have surprised me with the extent of their sharing. Several years ago, while on one of my many residential meditation courses, I found myself chatting during one of our meal breaks to a delightful lady who I met for the first time on that weekend. For some reason she chose to drop a little nugget of information into our conversation. It might help if I could remember what we were talking about at the time, however, I do remember that it had little to do with our chat, so I was genuinely surprised when she told me that she used to be a prostitute. Interesting. I had no idea why she felt the impulse to mention it but I was happy to go with the flow. I asked her if she enjoyed it at the time. She was clear in her response to the negative and told me that she had not liked herself very much then but it gave her a chance to control men.

It is no odds to me what she did then or what she is doing now, however I did wonder why she chose to tell me, so I asked her. She said that she felt safe telling me. Interesting. Safe from what? Safe from whom? What was I supposed to do with the information? I like to believe that she saw in me and understood from me that I held no judgement.

Then there was the time a couple of years ago on another course when one of the students, a propos of nothing, told me that she had lived in Amsterdam where she worked 'in the sex trade', as she put it. Interesting. Why was she choosing to tell me this? Why me indeed. I thought it best not to presume, as I know people who might consider serving behind the counter of an adult shop in Soho, as working 'in the sex trade'. When she confirmed that she did mean prostitution, I asked her how she felt about herself when she was doing it. As with anyone else I do not care what she did then or what she does now, all that matters is how she feels.

She thought about it and said, "Sometimes I didn't like myself very much and other times I despised myself."

"So do you feel better about yourself now?" She said yes and I was glad to hear it. Her life in prostitution had served her at a time when she had little joy in her relationships and no love to give or receive. Now she is learning to allow people to be kind and caring towards her instead of pushing them away. This was all very interesting and I wondered why she chose to tell me, so I asked her.

"Is this the kind of information you would normally give to someone you hardly know?" I was surprised to hear her say,

"I feel I know you well enough, I know you won't judge me."

Interesting.

*

Even though I do not actively encourage it, people seem to seek me out to pass information to me. There was the time I was standing at a bus stop in Ladbroke Grove waiting for the 295 after a failed hairdressing visit, which I will not go into right now. Anyway, a lady hobbled towards me with her walking stick. She could have stood nearby and waited for a bus like me but she stood in front of me and within seconds started to tell me about her hospital outpatients' appointments, her leg operations and her life now as a result of diminished mobility. She continued with facts about her change in diet and how she feels better for eating different foods, as well as how she wishes her leg would be better, so she could get out and about more. How interesting to receive such a lot of information from a stranger. The bus came, I boarded, she did not get on but walked away from the bus stop. So she was not even waiting for a bus but had just stopped to chat to me. How sweet.

*

Then there was the time I sat on the seat of a bus shelter waiting for a number 24 at the beginning of its route in Hampstead near the beautiful heath. I sat at one end of the long red seat which was easily long enough for six people. I had perched myself right at the end, the very end.

The remainder of the seat was free so imagine my amusement when a man approached and without so much as an introduction, he sat beside me. When I say sat beside me, I mean right beside me, so close that we were physically touching. Bearing in mind that the rest of the seat was empty, why did he sit so close? After all, this is London, people do not sit next to random others do they? To be fair, none of this occupied my mind at the time, I was happy, I was in a good emotional place, I had no concerns, it was his choice to sit beside me and that did not actually bother me. This is not to say that another time, another place, another seat, another person may not have led to a completely different reaction from me. Who knows? All I know is that on that day at that time I was not bothered. All was well.

I looked at him and smiled, he smiled back and straight away began telling me that he had just been to the hospital for this out patients' appointment, to check his progress following his surgery. He then seemed to take delight in telling me that he was looking forward to meeting his friends in the afternoon for lunch and how they were good friends but sometimes they failed to turn up, yet he was happy to arrange to meet them again, just because he liked their company.

47

He was a sweet little man and considering his presentation, I had a bit of a challenge to see him as healthy and thriving. He continued to talk, I continued to listen, then he stood up, wished me a lovely day and walked away. He was not even waiting for a bus, so why did he choose to sit beside me at the bus stop? Why indeed.

*

Then there was the Saturday afternoon when I waited for my wonderful daughter who was scheduled to emerge from Belsize Park tube station after a few minutes. It was a glorious sunny day and due to the heat, I sensibly decided to wait for her at the top of the hill rather than walk down to meet her, then for both of us to trudge back up it. At the top of the hill is a strategically placed bench. Good thinking from the council. A man sat at one end. I smiled at him as I approached and said,

"Hi, I'll just pop myself at the other end of this bench if I may."

He gestured in agreement and began speaking immediately about the beauty of the day, the gorgeousness of the weather, the warmth of the sun, his leisurely afternoon following his active morning busy on an allotment, for someone who employed him. I could not help but be a little surprised, as I was always under the impression that the whole point of an allotment is to grow the produce yourself, not to pay someone else to do it for you. Anyway, he had enjoyed his morning in nature but was glad to be resting.

He was an interesting man and readily told me about his several years of working in Greece where he thoroughly enjoyed the climate, much as we were experiencing in London on that day, when we found ourselves conversing so easily. So why did he leave the wonderful, reliable, warm climate of Greece? Sadly, because his work was not consistent and he needed the stability of regular income guaranteed back in London.

I actually do not remember how we progressed on to the subject of his wives, not one but two marriages that he was glad to be out of. It was interesting to see how his mood and demeanour altered when he changed the subject matter from sunny Greece to gloomy spouses. Still, it was not my emotion, so when my daughter arrived, I parted company from the talkative man on the bench and left him to his thoughts.

*

The vast majority of my talking to strangers experiences tend to occur when I am alone. I guess that makes sense. It is particularly significant when I remember occasions in the past when I have been out with a friend who complained or became quite upset when I have talked to a random other.

By way of example, I was out shopping with a chap who exhibited disturbingly unpleasant reactions when I attempted to have fun with restaurant and shop staff. Another time, I shopped with a female friend who she accused me of flirting when I joked with a server in a café. Another time, I went to the cinema with a female friend who lost her temper, accused me of showing off and sulked when I had a laugh with the ticket seller.

I have been accused of all sorts of other nonsense and of course, it used to upset me. So my response was to stop doing something I enjoyed, in my effort to please the person I was with, who from their place of insecurity did not feel comfortable with me being myself.

If I was to be joyful, something had to give. It was a simple choice really. I could try to please them or try to please myself, in the past I chose to put them first. Well, that is what we are taught is it not? We are taught not to be selfish right? We are taught to always put others first, to consider their feelings and their preferences before our own, are we not? So I was a good girl, I wanted to be liked, I wanted to be a good friend just like anyone else.

In an effort to please, I stopped talking to strangers because the person I was with felt uncomfortable. I discovered that there was a problem with that. I was not allowing myself to be me. Of course this aspect of my personality was not the only thing that I reduced in order to please others, it was just one of many traits which took a back seat. I learned to my cost that people were still not happy, so I was wasting my time anyway.

When I decided to put myself first, guess what? Bingo, I learned how to be happy. I did not need suffocating relationships anyway so I left them to be as they choose to be and now everyone wins.

*

So my experiences are usually when I am alone, I assume I see people and respond to them differently or more to the point they see me differently when I am alone. However I was out with my wonderful daughter walking along the Euston Road one Friday afternoon, when an unexpected interaction took place.

The timing was interesting because we were in the area for an appointment at the council offices, we had arrived a little early, were announcing our arrival at reception when I suddenly had the urge to go and do something else first. Without detailed explanation, I excused myself and taking my daughter with me we left the building. I followed my urge to pop to the post office and as we walked back to the council office, I felt better.

I was walking beside my daughter along the wide pavement of the ever busy Euston Road, opposite the beautiful picturesque St Pancras Station. It was a beautiful day, not that it mattered because I never much care what the weather chooses to do. It is only weather after all and I have some difficulty in understanding the notion of weather being good or bad. It just is as it is. Anyway, I was happy, all was well.

A distraction ensued. I noticed her just moments before she sprinted towards me diagonally across the crowded pavement. Who was she? I try to see the best in people, I try to see them as healthy and thriving and considering the way she presented herself, this was no small challenge. Regardless of her appearance, despite the initial impression and knowing nothing about her, I knew that seeing her well-being was the greatest gift I had to offer at that moment in time.

She stood before me, right in front of me, less than a metre away. My daughter, (bless her) continued to walk. I stopped. I did not try to move left or right, I stayed where I was. I did not need to wait, she began talking. She needed money to book into a hostel, she was homeless, had nowhere to stay and no food to eat. She spoke, I listened. Froth collected in the corners of her mouth and spray accompanied her words. I was not bothered. She thanked me for stopping she thanked me for listening. She smiled a brown stump smile. My daughter had returned but chose to maintain a discreet and healthy distance, well out of froth spraying range at least. Very wise.

The woman in front of me looked across at my first born and asked her if I was her mother. After the nod, she told her that I was a lovely lady to stop and help her by listening, no one ever listens to her, no one ever stops. She looked back at me and told me that my daughter was beautiful, she looked like me and we were both beautiful. For some reason her desperate need for money seemed to be less urgent, as she chose to tell me about her father, who had left her mother to live with a woman in Scotland and how they had a child, who was her half-sister and looked just like my daughter.

It was all very interesting but it was time to move on. I wished her well and we started to walk away. After a couple of paces, my daughter stopped, took a handful of pound coins out of her purse and walked back to the woman to put money in her hand. Interesting.

*

Then there was the morning I paid one of my regular visits to the traditional sweet stall in Covent Garden. I always enjoy a jovial exchange with the humorous owner in his white coat and bowler hat. This day was no exception and when I finished I turned to find a man standing right behind me. I thought he was waiting to buy something but he spoke to me,

"Hallo, I hope you don't mind me asking but I was wondering if you might be able to spare some change please, I need to get the bus and I don't have enough money."

Well, that was okay with me, I had coins in my hand from my purchase of bonbons so I gave them to him. He seemed happy enough and wanted to thank me. There was no need as I was just following my guidance in the moment and that is what I promised myself I will do, anytime and anywhere.

For instance, there was the Sunday I arrived in Bristol for a day of parent and child bonding with my wonderful daughter. Walking arm in arm along the street we passed a Big Issue seller who had the biggest smile and cheery face that brightened up the dull day. We walked past him as neither of us wanted a magazine but I felt the inspiration to go back and give him money and tell him it was just because I liked his happy face. He expressed such delight and gratitude that I was in danger of giving even more,

"Thank you very much, that is very kind of you, I really appreciate it, both of you have a lovely day."

*

There have been times when my nearest and dearest have expressed concerns about refusing requests for money from people in the street. They felt guilty and fearful so either gave money when they do not want to, or worried about not giving money, expecting retaliation from the requesting person or a vengeful higher force. Either way it is a not so good feeling emotion. I do not subscribe to such theories. I follow my guidance in the moment. I follow my gut instinct, call it what you like, if it feels right, I do it. As my counsellor used to say, *'if it feels good it is good, if it doesn't it isn't'*.

I have lived with a couple of significant influences who expressed fear of the wrath of gypsies, giving them all sorts of powers and abilities, whether true or not. I was walking on a busy street in our wonderful Central London on Friday lunchtime when I saw before me a group, a team, a clan, a gang, a gaggle, a collection of ladies offering sprigs of heather to passers-by. I saw people changing direction to avoid them. I saw people scurrying past to escape them. I saw people pretending not to see them. I saw people choosing not to respond when the ladies spoke to them. This was all well and good but none of it directly impacted on me.

I carried on walking when one of the ladies spotted me. She walked forwards and stood in front of me. I stopped, I smiled and perhaps it was my imagination but she looked surprised. She offered me a sprig of heather for good luck and without waiting for me to accept or decline her offer, she pushed it into the buttonhole of my coat. I thanked her and told her that I already have lots of good luck. She asked for money and I removed the heather telling her, that even though it was beautiful I was giving it back to her, so that she could give it to someone else in better need of her good luck charm.

She asked for money again anyway, well there is no harm in asking is there? I said, "I am not going to give you any money but I am going to give you my blessing and good wishes for a lovely day."

Well, I could have had no idea how she was going to react to that. I did not really mind either way, I was not worried about any repercussions as my sentiments were offered from the heart. I like to believe that on some level she knew that and was indeed responding to that when she said,

"God bless ya darlin', you have a lovely day too."

*

Interestingly, a couple of months later I was walking down the same road when a similar group of ladies occupied the same patch, as they conducted their familiar stop and ask, heather inspired activities. I took control of the conversation when one of them stopped me by asking her if she was the lady I had met before. Then I picked a name, any name out of the air and asked if someone by that name was part of the group.

"She's not here today, her boy is sick." I picked another name, a boy's name out of the air and she confirmed that was the name of the sick boy. She assumed I knew them but I did not, I had simply chosen random names. I said,

"Tell her I wish them both well."

She thanked me with a, "God love ya darlin' for bein' so kind" and off I went. To my surprise she insisted on giving me heather and a lucky pebble even though I declined her offer and gave no money. Interesting indeed.

*

This leads me neatly to another much loved group of people who regularly inhabit our streets, come rain or shine, dominating the pathways and requesting money for an ever changing variety of reasons.

I laugh when I look back at the dramatic change of my relationships with charity collectors over the years, now that I have dramatically changed my relationship with myself. Years ago, I was never stopped in the street. There could have been no one else about and they would still let me walk by. That was what I expected and that was what I got. There was something about me which prevented them from not wanting to speak to me. Sometimes I would see one of them look at me then look away. I did not know what their brief was. I had no idea of their training and what instructions they were given to choose prospective people to approach. Whatever their criteria, I did not fit it. After a considerable number of years of being invisible (and I do not mean in the Harry Potter magical cloak kind of way) things in my life began to turn around. My perspective changed, I learned about self-appreciation, which enhanced my self-esteem, improved my self-image and mountains began to move. Interestingly, as I changed, so did their attitude towards me. Suddenly or perhaps not so suddenly, I was in a different bracket, seemingly ticking different boxes on their list. Before I continue I am quite aware that the commonly accepted term of endearment for them is 'chuggers' however as I said in my previous book, this name does not resonate with me so others are free to use it if they wish.

I was accustomed to seeing people on the street with their clipboards. They used to be conducting surveys on all manner of products and lifestyle choices. As time progressed they became collectors for some charitable cause or another. The clipboards continued, identification cards arrived, as did t-shirts, with the name of their cause in the moment. More recently, the ID cards have increased in size and the matching t-shirts and jackets seem to be more elaborate in design. The collectors are even easier to spot from a distance.

An early experience with them was a few years ago. I was walking through Richmond, down George Street on a busy Saturday afternoon when I spotted a young, tall not to mention handsome man in a short brightly coloured jacket. Carrying a clipboard, he had a big smile that lit up his face. He walked across the pavement passing other people as he moved forward to stand in front of me.

I was new to the attention so was a little surprised to see him go to so much trouble. I did not need to be concerned as his opening line explained all,

"Hallo there, I saw you coming down the road and I thought that you looked like such a nice lady, I decided I really wanted to talk to you."

Well, that was such a lovely opening line. After a quick question from me, he attempted to assure me that no, he certainly does not say that to everyone. In turn, I attempted to assure him that I would not be handing over any money and he laughed. He surprised me by saying that he was so happy to talk to me, that he did not even want to talk about the charity, if I did not want to. He looked at me warmly with his gorgeous, smiling face and said that he would happily talk about anything that interested me as long as I stayed.

Well, well, well, that was good enough for me. I was not about to complain, oh no. I thought I was fairly happy before he stopped me but his words succeeded in helping me to feel happier still. I stayed, we chatted, I did not stay very long but long enough to enjoy his flattery and attention a little further and to indulge myself with more opportunity to enjoy the beauty of his handsome features. I announced my departure and amidst his protestations, thanked him for being such a lovely young man and for making a lady very happy.

Since that memorable moment I have been treated to a plethora of enjoyable experiences with charity clipboard contribution collectors. There has been such a turnaround in expectation that it makes me laugh sometimes to think about it. In the past I was never approached and I learned to never expect it. Little did I know that it is the expectation which comes first. This is just something else which I have thankfully learned.

*

A couple of years ago I had been to one of my regular Friday morning meditation meetings in London's beautiful, lively, wonderful Covent Garden. I found myself enjoying this weekly routine with joy and excitement every week for about a year and a half. I often questioned the sanity of leaving my warm comfortable bed with my cuddly teddy bears so early, to leave my home before six in the morning, to bus my way into town. My motives and intentions were all the more questionable when the cold, dark, wintery morning was the backdrop for my journey. For some reason, I never doubted myself for long and whatever the weather I would feel like skipping to the bus stop in anticipation of the meeting. Whether I shared the meeting with two people or ten, I would always leave the venue in a good feeling emotional place.

So on this particular Friday, I was walking about pretending to live in Central London, which is one of my favourite activities. This is a fact I shared with a market stall holder once, who expressed his astonishment when I told him how much I love and would adore to live in this part of the capital. He was indignant with his opinion about how deluded and confused I must be. He had much to say about traffic, crowds, smells, transport, prices, property, service and more. I listened half-heartedly as not much of what he said resonated with me. He tried to assure me that I must be wrong and could not possibly want to live somewhere so lacking in positive qualities.

Anyway, back to my day in question. I was strolling across Leicester Square when a young, casually dressed, smiling, young, chirpy chappy sprinted towards me. It was a dull day but he appeared like a ray of sunshine, seemingly full of delight and asked if I could spare a couple of minutes to chat to him. Well, as soon as I looked at him I was captivated. It is always a source of wonder and joy to me as I am reminded of the way we rendezvous with wonderful people when we feel wonderful.

I could try to describe the beauty of his gorgeous eyes but words have not yet been invented, which could adequately convey the feeling I enjoyed as I gazed into the windows of his soul. They were bright, so very bright and not blue but grey. His eyes were grey and as he allowed me to stare into them, I felt as if I could see into forever. They were the most magnificent eyes ever beheld. I tried to describe them to a friend and said, "I could see into infinity." Well apparently, according to him, I cannot say that. I suppose that is the price I pay for using the word 'infinity' in an eye gazing context when talking to a mathematician.

Anyway, the eyes had my attention. I was easily willing to spare a couple of minutes, perhaps a couple of lifetimes given the opportunity. I am not one to shy away from paying compliments. For me it is simply a way of acknowledging beauty when I see it. The way I felt at the time, it was not really like I had any choice. He had started to speak and I found it impossible to listen, as I was totally distracted by those eyes. My head seemed to involuntarily tilt as I lost myself and the gazing continued.

I told him I was distracted and I told him why. He was fine about it and just carried on talking. We chatted but not about his charity. We somehow stumbled upon the subject of modern dance, contemporary expression, interpretation of life and tattoos. He asked if I had any tattoos, I told him no. He told me he has some. I did not feel inclined to ask to see them. Our conversation about body illustrations lasted longer than I would normally expect, given that I do not have any and have no intention of changing that aspect of my personal physical expression. For some reason this charming gentleman even found himself telling me the names and locations of famous body ink artistes.

We soon progressed to chatting about the fast approaching St Valentine's Day, which was the following week. He seemed happy to talk about his girlfriend and his plans and I soon discovered that I was enjoying the company of a genuine romantic. He was a poet and had written poetry for her. Not just that, he had written lots of poems for her on separate pieces of different coloured paper, which he had put into a large empty sweetie jar. Oh my goodness, how romantic is that? I was delighted for her and I said so. He hoped that she would like it and I excitedly told him that, whether she did or not, I thought it was a wonderfully romantic and thoughtful thing to do and that there are many women who would simply adore the effort and attention he had obviously put into such a gift.

Well, as if there was not enough, he bowled me over by saying that he was also planning to bake a cake for her, with pink icing. What a super, super guy. I am aware that these displays are not welcomed by everyone. I appreciate that some people may think differently to me. I understand the response, 'makes me want to barf' from some people when I shared this story but none of that matters. The lovely romantic man liked telling me and I liked hearing it.

He made some unnecessary apology about not having much money to celebrate his love for her and yet I would have struggled to be more excited for her. I could never know if she was going to gratefully receive and appreciate his gestures but I know I did. My children (bless them) did not totally agree with my reaction and that is fine too. Their interpretation of his proposed action or intentions did not put me off at all. I loved it, all of it and I am still happy for the lady at the receiving end of his displays of affection. In fact I am pleased for them both.

After such a wonderful uplifting conversation, did we talk about the charity? Not much.

*

Every now and again I remember how wonderful my life is now that I enjoy such freedom to be myself. Every now and again I remember how different my interactions used to be. There was never any expectation of a stranger talking to me, I had tried smiling but got nothing back, perhaps I might have occasionally received a scowl or a glare or other expression of disapproval from people for no apparent reason it seemed. I became accustomed to poor service in shops and restaurants too. My memories of leaving places following rudeness from staff are plentiful. I felt hard done by. I was hard done by. My life was miserable in so many ways. I took little pleasure in going out and meeting people as so often my disappointment, frustration or some kind of misunderstanding became too much. Time after time it was just too much. I realised that my emotional state was unsustainable, I was miserable and lonely and something had to be done.

A few years ago something happened. I made the decision that I wanted things to be different. I wanted my life to be different. I discovered that life is supposed to be fun. I understood that the task of changing significant aspects of my life would take time and effort. I knew it would be worth it. My personal work had begun and results were beginning to reveal themselves.

Among other things I wanted to change the outcome of my interactions with people I did not know, so I made the conscious decision to actively improve my experiences in that arena. One day I went out with a goal in mind, to see if I could get one person to smile at me. Just one smile would be enough. So, I set the intention to smile at people and continue to smile at them whether they smiled back or not.

The first time I received the gift of a smile from a stranger in the street, I was delighted. I returned home feeling quite successful indeed. One smile was achieved and I decided to up the stakes and go for the triple. Before long, I received the gift of three smiles from three strangers in the same day. I had found the courage to smile at people and it was paying off. Well, things were looking good and I was feeling good. Were they responding to me in a positive way? It certainly felt like it and I liked it. I wanted more of it. I did not want to be greedy but once I had succeeded in my total of three, I set the intention to double it. Perhaps I had gone too far, perhaps I was being ridiculous, perhaps but there was only one way to find out.

I did it! Six smiles in one day, yay! I hit the jackpot and I have not looked back since. The amazing thing is that I am now so used to people smiling readily at me, that I cannot remember when I made the transition, from them smiling in response to me, to me smiling in response to them. Either way, who cares? It is a continual exchange of energy, a continual exchange of gifts. A smile is a pleasure to give, a joy to receive and I have come to understand and appreciate how each one is shared. The benefits of a smile ripple out to every person we meet and everyone they meet, affecting everyone, yes, the whole universe. Never underestimate the power of a smile. It has the power to change the emotion of the receiver from a place of 'nobody loves me' to 'somebody cares'. We never know what someone is going through when we pass in the street and that smile can speak volumes.

Phew, that is probably enough about the power of a smile for now. Moving on.

*

Back to charity clipboarders, to a time I wandered peacefully down Neal Street in Covent Garden in London, (probably) the best city in the world, when I saw a group of them doing their thing. A young man with thick, black, curly hair in cute little plaits, skipped towards me and jumped in front of me with a big beaming smile. His playful activity and happy face made me laugh. I found it cute to see the way he approached me, so when he asked if I had time to listen to a few words about his charity, I felt inclined to give him some of my attention to hear him speak.

He started, he spoke, I listened, he asked a couple of obvious questions requiring a definite yes or no answer. I was amused by the style as the questions were so cleverly worded, that anyone who was still listening would have given the same response I guess. The rest of the time he spoke and spoke and spoke some more. At one point I wondered if he had realised that we were not actually having a conversation, he was just talking at me. Perhaps that was the intention. Anyway, I was in no hurry, I had no pressing engagement, he was pleasant enough to look at, so I allowed him to continue.

His pitch was about the plight of families, education, health, water and everyday situations in a faraway place. After what seemed like several minutes (it probably was not but certainly felt like it) he paused. I waited. His last line was something about looking for people willing to give regular donations for the help they promised to give. I said,

Carole Chandler

"Not today thank you."

He paused, lowered his clipboard, continued to look at me and said,

"May I ask why not?"

My guidance was to say, "Because it does not inspire me." He paused again, I continued to smile and continued to wait.

He said, "May I ask what does inspire you?"

"Lots of things."

"Would you mind telling me what some of them are?"

"Thank you for asking but I don't need you to approve of them for me to feel better."

With that he smiled and held out his hand to shake mine and said,

"I understand. I can see that you are clearly someone who has their equanimity in check."

"Ooh, my equanimity is in check is it, I think I like the sound of that." To be honest, I was not absolutely certain what he meant by the use of that particular word but it sounded positive to me and that was good enough.

"Yes, it's a compliment, I can see you are balanced."

Well that was lovely for me to hear too. I thanked him, we wished each other a good day and parted.

*

Then there was the Tuesday lunchtime when I walked from Wimbledon shopping centre towards the train station. A lively young lady wearing a huge white padded jacket appeared before me with her clipboard, waving an oversized identity card clipped to a lanyard around her neck. She wanted to talk to me about the demise of the snow leopard and she thought I had a kind face and I looked like a giver, so she hoped I might have time to listen.

She made me smile. Her big curly hair bounced and seemed to have a life of its own. So much hair moving continually as she spoke. I allowed her to deliver her pitch uninterrupted and at the end she asked the question about willingness to give details for regular donations. My response was,

"No thank you, not today."

For some reason she jumped backwards and throwing her arms up in the air she shouted,

"I've never met anyone as calm as you before." I smiled, she continued,

"People normally get angry with me and tell me to go away." Poor girl, never mind, I wished her a lovely day and left.

About thirty seconds down the road I spotted a young, tall, neat man sporting a white padded jacket holding his clipboard and waving an equally oversized identity card clipped to a lanyard around his neck. He too expressed a desire to educate me about the reducing snow leopard population, had noticed me approaching in the crowd and thought I would be happy to stop and listen.

Well let's be honest, I was unlikely to hear anything I had not heard seconds before but I was intrigued by the name he presented before me on his ID card. I asked him about it. He told me the origin, he also seemed happy to tell me about his upbringing in Greece and his Nigerian parents, who still live there and how he loves to visit, as the weather is so great and how he should visit them more often and how he has not decided where he wants to live and what he wants to do after he finishes his studies.

What about the charity? I told him that the pretty bouncy girl with the beautiful bouncy hair had already told me everything. I was about to leave but when he said that it was his first day and that I had helped him to feel better by stopping, I decided to give him a couple of minutes of my time to practise his pitch on me. Oh what fun. He seemed to enjoy the opportunity and my life was not adversely affected by the interaction so why not?

A few weeks later I saw the same chap on Streatham High Street, outside the library, different jacket, different charity, different ID card, same name. I recognised him and reminded him of our Wimbledon conversation. He seemed delighted to be recognised, bless him.

*

Then there was the time I walked down Neal Street again (well I do spend a lot of time in Covent Garden) when a chap wearing a colourful tabard and carrying a red bucket asked me for a donation for something or other. I cannot remember how but for some reason or another we had a conversation about peace, tranquillity and fasting for Ramadan. Why did he tell me he was fasting? Who knows? We had a pleasant chat anyway.

About a three weeks later I saw the same lovely guy on Putney High Street, collecting money, wearing a tabard, carrying perhaps the same or another red bucket. I have no idea how but he recognised me, his face lit up when he saw me and when I doubted him he said that he remembered where and when we met and even our conversation. How is that even possible, I ask myself? Not hundreds but thousands of people must have passed him on that busy thoroughfare that is Neal Street. Never mind, who am I to question his powers of recall? Perhaps I am memorable after all.

This reminds me of the time I paused by a stall in the Covent Garden covered market. It is such a wonderfully lively place for browsing and shopping for Londoners, visitors and tourists all day and every day. I stopped by a stall selling beautiful, contemporary, silver jewellery pieces. I had previously noticed a gorgeous, wide, dimpled bangle and just idly wondered if it was still there. The trader sat on a stool as I browsed and said,

"Hallo, I remember you, I've seen you here before."

Well, if that were true I would have been flattered indeed, however, I very much doubted it, as it had been easily four weeks since I had passed his particular stall and I repeat, not hundreds but thousands of people flow constantly through the market area. Most of the stall holders are hardly paying attention to anyone, never mind have time to remember little me.

Apparently I was wrong. He declared that he remembered me because I looked at the same bangle and he recognised my own jewellery and he had seen me about a month ago. Okay, he convinced me, so who was I to doubt his powers of recall? Perhaps I was memorable after all.

Not bad eh? Not bad coming from someone who was told many years ago that she was easily forgettable. I was told by a man who I respected, a work colleague, that I was the kind of person who people liked when they saw me but instantly and forgot about me once I had gone. What was his reason for sharing this view? Who knows? Who cares? I did. I cared a lot. It hurt. It really hurt. I did not know why it hurt so much then. I understand now. I know better now. I understand why limiting beliefs are detrimental to our well-being. I have let go of this limiting belief and many others and guess what? Now I am having a far better time. Whether I am remembered or not is inconsequential, now I just feel so much better about myself and being remembered is a bonus.

*

Over the years I have had a great deal of fun with the charity chaps. When they began stopping me I was surprised and then I became used to it. For a while I would say right at the beginning that I did not need or want to hear their pitch because I had no intention of giving any money. I did not much like the way that went, so I changed my response.

I decided to listen for a bit before interrupting them, to ask whether they might be willing to consider an alternative approach to restoring their view of world order. I would mention universal law, however, surprise surprise, some of them were not keen on the suggestion of an alternative perspective, especially one which appears so simplistic. I did not much like the way some of those conversations went, so I changed my response.

For a while now I have been enjoying my current M.O. They stop me, I smile, they talk, I listen, they request, I gratefully, politely and respectfully decline their invitation to join whatever concern they happen to be supporting and the interactions go much better. Interestingly, I am no longer met by representatives who are, how shall I put it, less than polite, less than charming, less than charitable.

The lesson for me has been to learn how to stay in my secure emotional space and not allow myself to be drawn in by them, no matter how much guilt they may try to dump my way, when no money is offered. Each and every one of us has the freedom to think as we choose and do as we choose.

Bless them all for trying and they certainly add to the variety that is life, but it is no-one's business to judge what another decides to do with 'just the price of a cup of coffee'.

*

Then there was the chap wearing a sky blue jacket carrying a matching umbrella in Wimbledon High Street. He invited me to join him as protection from the rain. This was sweet of him and he introduced himself, taking my hand then continued to hold it as he began talking about saving some group from something somewhere. I thanked him and asked for my hand to be returned, as I did not want to hear more about his charity, even though he had gorgeous eyes and I would normally be more than happy to gaze into them and lose myself for a while.

Then there was the exuberant, jolly, lively, young lad on Camden High Street, who had a crop of curly hair that was just crying out to have my fingers run through it but I restrained myself. I managed to easily distract him from his pitch when for some reason, (I have no idea why) I asked him why he was doing the charity stuff for work and whether that was his lifelong ambition. Like that was not possibly impudent enough, I also asked him what he really wanted to do with his life and what was stopping him from doing it.

After a pause he seemed happy to share that even though he appeared to be cheerful, the charity work was depressing him, he was tired of the rejection, negativity and rudeness from people, he also doubted the effectiveness of his actions too. He just wanted to be happy. I confirmed the benefits of his search for joy. He really wanted to travel to South America to visit the Amazon rainforest and the river. He had been thinking about it more and more and said that our conversation was inspiring him to 'just do it'. He thanked me, bless him.

Carole Chandler

Life is great, I meet such wonderful people. Now when I see charity clipboarders in the high street, I actually look forward to the interaction, I have fun and they seem to enjoy it as well. Every time is an opportunity for me to practise improving my ability to focus, to practise maintaining my balance, to practise allowing myself to be me and allowing others to be as they choose to be, to think as they choose to think and to do as they choose to do.

*

Then there was the chap on the Northcote Road in Clapham Junction who tried to stop me as I walked towards my bus stop. I said that I was happy to listen but I was not interested in interrupting my journey so invited him to join me and said,

"Come with me, let's walk and talk."

His protestations did not concern me much, as he tried to say something about not being allowed to walk with me for legal reasons. Never mind, I do not suppose for a moment that I missed very much by not giving him more of my time. Another day, another place it could have all gone differently.

Another day another clipboarder on the same road voiced his concerns about accepting my invitation to walk and talk, telling me that they are not allowed to take more than three steps. I suggested that his maths may need some attention as he had already walked past a few shops with me. He defended himself by saying that he is studying maths at university then said he can say what he likes to produce the results that he wants. I was intrigued because he sounded like he was talking about mathematics in a spiritual sense. What a fascinating man.

*

Then there was the feisty older gentleman collecting on behalf of his cause for concern in Clapham Junction. His somewhat confrontational opening line inspired me to simply say that I was not aware of the events he mentioned. Evidently, this was not the response he expected and he made no attempt to hide his surprise, when I said that I do not read the papers, watch or listen to the news. He seemed discontent and asked about my knowledge of current affairs closer to home. I happily admitted that I only pay attention to events which inspire me, otherwise I let it be. He started to say, "But you must ..." and for some reason decided not to continue. His look of disbelief did not bother me in the slightest as I had not asked for his approval and I did not need it.

Perhaps years ago I might have been embarrassed to tell anyone that I did not keep abreast of world situations, good or bad. Thankfully those days are long gone, far far away. Now that I understand and know the benefits of choosing my perspective, choosing what I give my attention to, choosing what I focus on, I am mindful of avoiding bad news and negative issues. I have learned that if we give any attention to something unwanted we get more of it. In an effort to influence my ability to be positive, my early choices had to be drastic so reading newspapers, watching news channels and listening to the radio on the half hour were among the first things to be eliminated.

Carole Chandler

This made a massive difference and was not as easy as it may sound particularly when living with other people who insist on remaining 'informed'. Yes, people were not comfortable with my decision at first but my intentions were clear and now they are used to it. Now this continues to be a major choice, I am me and this is what I prefer.

*

Then there was the Thursday lunchtime I walked from Victoria station towards Parliament Square. Just before the main shopping area, I spotted a large group of collectors and one of them spotted me. This is a high pedestrian traffic area especially at that time of day and I was in a crowd of fast moving people, on my way to returning a recent purchase to a branch of House of Fraser.

I saw this guy notice me because it was comical to see him weave through the crowd towards me. It was hard to ignore his gorgeous handsome face with a smile of radiance and joy. His silver and black hair complemented his glowing, coffee coloured skin and his little beard looked neat and recently trimmed. He was a joy to behold, so when he stopped in front of me, smiled and held out his hand, I could think of no immediate reason not to accept the offer of a handshake.

He introduced himself, mentioned his charity then launched straight in with detailed information about who he was supporting, why he was supporting them and their plans for the necessary assistance. Wow, he was an eloquent speaker, his motivation seemed clear and sincere and I enjoyed listening to him. I must have been comfortable because it was some time before I noticed that he was still holding my hand with both of his hands.

I thought it only reasonable to ask, "May I have my hand back now please?"

He feigned surprise and released his grasp, then carried on talking and I continued to listen. He seamlessly changed from talking about his cause, to complimenting me, expressing lovely views about my appearance, my demeanour, my personality and somehow before I realised it, he was holding my hand again. How did he even do that? Quite a skill I think.

The pitch and the compliments had to come to an end and he seemed totally unconcerned when I thanked him for the work he was doing, congratulated him on his obvious passion for his occupation and said that I did not intend to financially support it. It was nice of him to say that he had enjoyed meeting me and talking to me. He thanked me for my time and I was ready to leave when he said,

"Oh wait, I didn't ask your name."

"It's Carole."

"Ah, lovely to meet you and have a great day, Empress Carole."

"Ooh, Empress Carole. I like that, I could get used to that."

"Yes, it is clear that you are an Empress."

Wow, what a wonderful interaction.

I told this little tale to a friend, who seemed to enjoy it as much as I did. It inspired her to do some investigating of her own. When we next met she gave me a card on which she had written, 'Empress – she who sets in order'. Interesting.

One little thing that I also found interesting was that the day I met him, I went to the store as intended and returned about ten minutes later to find that the whole group had disappeared. It was the same busy lunchtime but none of them were anywhere to be seen. Well it interested me anyway.

*

It would be easy to assume that people who spend their days hanging around on pavements stopping random pedestrians are a prime source of talking to strangers experiences. Yes that is true, however I am also aware that the many chats I have had with them and the few that I have shared here, are quite different to those experienced by others. Additionally, I have been surprised by people just chatting to me for no apparent reason.

There was the Wednesday morning I walked towards a bus stop near my home. The beginning of my route takes me through a residential area and sometimes there are people about, sometimes not. On this particular day, a woman approached me, smiled and instead of walking past she stopped.

"Hallo, I've seen you walking up and down this road and I told a neighbour that I wanted to meet you."

Well, that was a lovely thing for her to say and even lovelier for me to hear. To think that someone had seen me and thought nice things about me and said nice things about me and even wanted to meet me. Just another demonstration that we never know what another person may be thinking about us. We touch each other by our presence whether we are aware of it or not. She then stepped closer and raising her left hand she said,

"I really like your hair, it's so beautiful," while at the same time she stroked the right side of my head. There I was in the street being stroked by a woman I have never met before in my life. Was I bothered? Not so much. I imagine she must have felt pretty comfortable talking to me because she lowered her hand and stroked my upper arm as she carried on talking. I was still not bothered. I did not mind her telling me that she thought I was beautiful and I did not mind her telling me that she was happy to meet me.

What can I say? It was an interesting and joyful start to my day. I did not know who she was then and I do not know now. That happened about two years ago, I still live in the same place and walk along that same road several times a week and have never seen her again.

*

Then there was the day I walked along another road not so far from my home. I remember the day well, as it was early January and we had just enjoyed a recent fall of snow, so the pavements were artistically decorated in layers of white ice. I had just turned off Garratt Lane and from my perspective I was walking slowly, tentatively, looking down and concentrating. Never mind my emotional balance I was really concentrating to maintain my physical balance. I had no desire to end up sitting on the pavement. I looked down so hard that I had not seen a man walking towards me. The first I knew of his presence was when he interrupted my concentration by saying,

"Hey, that's a lovely smile, did you just win the lottery?"

I looked up to see the face of a gorgeous, handsome man wearing a radiant smile. I was happy for him to compliment me but failed to see how I could have possibly been smiling at all, considering my intense attention to each small step on the ice below. His lovely face distracted me enough to inspire me to say that I planned to win the lottery any time soon. He went on to tell me that he thought I was beautiful and had noticed me walking towards him. As he introduced himself, he asked my name, took my hand and held it saying,

"Well beautiful Carole, happy new year and I hope you get everything you wish for."

Wow, what a fabulous interaction that was. Fancy that, a total stranger going to so much trouble to wish me well. I thanked him, I was grateful, I appreciated it.

That happened over a year ago, on a road where I walk a few times a week and I have never seen him again.

*

Then there was the day I walked to work, a little further from my home this time on a warm sunny day. By the roundabout on the junction of Blackshaw Road and Plough Lane, I noticed a woman walking towards me. I found myself admiring her beauty, her hair was neatly scraped back into a cute little bun, her clothes looked really good on her slim frame and she walked elegantly in her suede ankle boots. I thought to myself that she looked beautiful and as she walked past she said,

"Lovely face." I was not sure that I heard her correctly. We both paused as I said,

"Excuse me?" She made a circle around her face with her hand, pointed at me and said,

"I was just saying that you have a lovely face."

"Oh thank you, that is very kind of you to say so and that's exactly what I was thinking about you."

For me this was just another indication that we get back what we give out. Some call it karma. I love knowing that when we think happy thoughts we attract happy things.

*

Then there was the time I walked further along this same route (well it is my route to work so I am there a lot) on an even warmer day and from a distance I noticed a lady in white trousers, white camisole and a floaty white chiffon type shirt with pink, pale blue and green patterns on it. I remember thinking that she looked like a beautiful butterfly as the breeze caught the fabric of her top and it wafted as she walked.

I was quite content thinking my happy thoughts to myself as we approached each other, when instead of passing by she stopped in front of me and said,

"Hallo, I like your hair." Well, that was very nice of her. It is always lovely to be complimented and this was no exception. I used to be terrible at accepting compliments, always suspecting ulterior motives, sarcasm or insincerity. I just adore it now and lap them up without question. I have often maintained that it means a lot to be complimented by men but even more when women not only think nice things about other women but actually go to the trouble and effort of saying lovely things to each other. There is something truly special about that. I am not talking about me because I am fully aware that my propensity to compliment others may be considered as perhaps, maybe, possibly a little above average.

Anyway the two of us chatted for several minutes, right there on the pavement of Plough Lane just along the road from the Shell petrol station. She was really quite delightful and it turned out that she loved my hair because I leave it natural. Well, this small aspect of my appearance has been the subject of many an interaction but more about some of those later.

She told me that she had decided to stop colouring her own hair, prompted by a comment made by her daughter. Oh bless our children. Her daughter had expressed herself as only a loving, secure, independent, self-aware, caring, young lady could,

"Mummy, stop dying your hair, it looks ridiculous." Well, what can I say? It shows the huge change in generations and attitudes but that is probably a conversation for another day.

Back to my butterfly lady, she heard her daughter and followed her suggestion. She was initially concerned about how she would cope with grey hair. Well, I know we had only just met but I was not going to let her get away with that. I stopped her in her tracks and told her what I tell everyone,

"It's not grey, it's silver." She did what most people do, she changed her expression as if recognising something that used to be familiar, was forgotten and now remembered and said,

"Oh yeah."

I said, "There, that feels better doesn't it?"

"Yes it does, it really does."

I continued, "It's all about perspective."

Everything is about perspective, as a wise person once said, *'when we change the way we look at things, the things we look at change'.*

Allow me to indulge myself for a moment while I give an example of how a difference of perspective can alter an impression of something. I have a choice, I could offer a serious example or a frivolous one. I have decided to go with frivolous. I was with my daughter enjoying some parent child bonding time, on a Thursday evening in Bristol. Looking for a suitable place to eat, we passed a restaurant that looked lovely inside, beautifully decorated, twinkly lights and lots of people. I saw a line of men and women standing inside, with their backs against the glass wall as we walked by, so I said to my daughter,

"Ooh look there's a choir." She looked around and asked me where I had seen them.

"In that restaurant, there, look, people are singing." It was November so it seemed quite reasonable to me until she said,

"No mummy, that's a queue, they're reading menus." We had a laugh and I thought it perfectly demonstrated the power of perspective. I am still happy to believe that they were singing from their music sheets, so that is the image I shall continue to hold in my mind.

So back to my beautiful, friendly, natural haired lady in the street. Our lovely lively chat continued and I felt like I had known her for ages. She expressed surprise at how she looked and felt younger with her hair natural. Well she did look lovely. She went on to tell me that she was even more surprised by the response from the men she was meeting socially. She said they really liked it and she was receiving far more attention since she stopped colouring it. Well, she was making an obvious but often ignored discovery. I pointed out that the men were responding to her joy and newly found confidence. Now that she was so pleased with herself, of course they were responding well, of course they were more attracted to her. Who would not be happy to meet someone who is happy to be themself and not fuss about stuff.

By the end of our conversation we said goodbye like old friends with a lovely long hug, well wishes and waves as we parted. She really was quite delightful.

*

Like I said, there have been numerous hair related conversation starters, like the chat I had with a lady I met who was behind the till in the supermarket on Tooting Broadway beneath South Thames College. While checking my purchases, she said she liked my hair and of course I thanked her and expected that to be it. She then stopped and told me that she would love to 'go natural' but did not think she was brave enough to stop the whole regular perming thing. I understood. I have been there. I offered the suggestion that she could perhaps try it and always choose to grow it again if she wished. Then I found out that her decision was a little more complicated than that. Even if she did find the courage, apparently, her husband definitely would not like it and he would probably leave her if she cut it short.

At the risk of getting carried away, I shall acknowledge that there is much that could be said about a relationship, where the hair choice of one is dictated by the preference of the other. At this moment I shall say no more.

Anyway, I probably did not need to be concerned for her as she said,

"Well, he is in Nigeria at the moment so maybe while he's away..." We both laughed and I resisted the temptation to say 'go girl'.

The conversation was fun but the thing that got me, was that she stopped working to talk to me and with people behind me waiting to pay for their shopping, I thought that was just a tad risky. For some reason, not one person complained. People are pretty vocal in this area, I live here, I have heard them, yet on this occasion, not a peep. Interesting.

*

Then there was the time I was pushing my trolley across the supermarket car park in Hounslow of all places, when a woman came running towards me shouting,

"Hallo, stop, stop wait, I want to ask you something!" She seemed eager about something, she was really running. What could she possibly want to ask me? Puffing and panting she thanked me for stopping,

"I like your hair, I wanted to see your hair. Did you do it yourself?"

"Do it myself? Do what myself?"

"The grey, the grey is lovely, did you put the grey in yourself?"

After I put her straight with the necessary it's-not-grey-it's-silver response, I wondered if she were actually insane to think that I had coloured it myself. I mean really, why would I do that? Frankly, I think I am an unusual individual enough as it is to leave my hair natural. How unusual would I be, to have black hair and add silver to it? Anyway, apparently she thought it was lovely and would love to do the same to her own hair but did not feel brave enough. There was that 'brave' thing again.

I know that I am used to strangers talking to me and it would be easy to forget how unusual some of these circumstances are. However, I confess that the being-chased-across-the-car-park scenario is a little 'out there' even for me.

Or so I thought, until it happened again. Believe it or not, a few months later while carrying my shopping back to the car in a supermarket car park, this time in Chiswick, a woman ran towards me calling out and approaching at speed. I did not quite know what to make of it, and then was amused when she too opened the dialogue with compliments about my hair. Blow me if she did not ask the same question,

"Did you put the grey in yourself?"

I am still more than a little surprised that anyone would even ask that. There is a multimillion pound industry aimed at persuading women to resist their natural hair colour and the loss of melanin is depicted as one of life's great beauty destroyers. The mere fact that I choose not to buy into that particular form of brainwashing, makes me a maverick in some ways but to go as far as to sprinkle my hair with silver dye to create my pepper and salt look, would be quite an individual choice to make. Anyway we had much the same conversation as the other supermarket car park chasing, hair lover and we parted happily.

Wonders never cease.

*

I have been known to follow the irresistible urge to talk to a stranger about their hair on more than one occasion. Several years ago I remember sitting on a number 33 bus travelling through Richmond. I had begun my personal improvement journey and had only limited experience with openly expressing the beauty I saw around me. In front of me sat a woman with the most beautiful curls I had ever seen. Her thick, dark brown, silky, shoulder length hair seemed to shine brightly and I felt unable to look anywhere but the back of her head.

The urge to say something was strong but at the time I was far more concerned about how she might react if I, a stranger on a bus, were to speak to her, just out of the blue like that. I thought about it long and hard and played different scenarios in my head about how the response may be, good or bad or worse still to suffer the shame of being ignored.

Like I said, it was several years ago, I was on my path but still had a lot to learn. I had not yet understood the importance of not needing approval from anyone, not anyone other than myself. Anyway, remaining totally distracted by the glowing locks, I concluded that I would probably regret it if I did not say anything. I decided that I wanted to give a compliment to make me feel good and I let go of any attachment to whatever her response may be. Of course, if she had disembarked before me then the whole inner dialogue would have been wasted but she remained in her seat as I stood up to leave. I plucked up the courage to stand beside her and say,

Carole Chandler

"Excuse me, I hope you don't mind but I did not want to get off the bus without telling you that your hair is absolutely beautiful."

She smiled a heart-warming, gorgeous smile and thanked me. Oh how silly of me. Why did I waste so much time and energy doubting that she would be anything other than pleased? Of course she was delighted, who would not be? Well that is the question. Why did I have so many experiences of compliments being thrown back in my face so many years ago? Now I understand how the world works, now it all makes sense. Before jumping off the bus I told her that I had been admiring her glorious hair for the entire journey and how beautiful I thought her curls were. She seemed happy and I know I was. It was a huge step for me and I was glad that I had the courage to take it.

*

Make no mistake, it is not only curly hair which catches my eye. While walking along Cross Deep in Twickenham one Saturday afternoon, I spotted a woman, wearing a long blue dress and she had very dark brown, straight hair down the full length of her back. It was clearly in excellent condition with straight strands smooth as silk like an elegant veil evenly cut at the bottom and totally had my attention.

I quickened my pace to afford myself a closer look. She walked at a leisurely speed so I easily caught up with her. I slowed down to enjoy admiring her hair as I walked behind her, then made the decision to share my joy with her. Speeding up to walk beside her I thought I would be the one to speak first but when she saw me looking at her, she immediately smiled and said, "Hallo." Well, I was not expecting that. I did not expect her to greet me, she did not even seem to wonder what I wanted, she just seemed comfortable to let me walk beside her. Gone are the days when I was met with, "what do you want?" "why are you so close?" or "who are you looking at?"

What I also did not expect was her dark skin. I guess that went some way to explaining the thick, glossy, long, straight, brown black hair. What I also did not expect was to see her in ecclesiastical clothing. She was a nun. Well, that was a surprise. She cheerfully received my compliments about her hair and about how much I enjoyed walking behind her and how I just wanted to tell her what I thought before I dashed off.

So those are a couple of people I have initiated interactions with a long time ago about their hair but I can truthfully say that I have never been inspired to chase anyone across a car park to talk to them about their hair or for any other reason come to think of it.

*

So my hair has been the subject of short and longer meetings. I was taking a stroll up the hill of Burntwood Lane in Earlsfield, on my way to Wandsworth Common just to enjoy the weather and the beauty of nature. I stopped to cross one of the side streets which is often busy as motorists use it as a cut through, parallel with the even busier Trinity road thus avoiding the traffic lights.

I stopped and the first car pulled up short, I thought to allow me to cross. The driver then changed her mind, drove forward a little, opened her window, waved a hand out of the window and shouted,

"Hey, I just had to stop and tell you that I think your hair is beautiful."

Well, that was certainly very kind of her to go to so much trouble but I was even more surprised because with three cars waiting behind her, she carried on speaking,

"Yes, it's lovely, I really love the way the colours suit you."

I thanked her again. I was convinced that had to be the end, for after all we were in London and drivers are not known for patience or even tolerance much of the time. It would be fair to expect some aggravation from one of the other drivers if she continued to hold up the queue, right? I was wrong. She wanted to tell me more from her car and shouted,

"I wish my hair was like yours. I would love to do mine like that but I don't think I've got the nerve." I quickly suggested that she could try it and see. Her parting words were, "You're beautiful," and off she drove.

That was a wonderful brief meeting and a great thing to happen while out on a walk. I am still surprised by the absence of open complaint from the drivers behind her. The whole event made me smile. She enjoyed my hair. I enjoyed her saying so. We enjoyed the interaction. Everyone was happy.

*

Then there was the time I crossed the traffic lights of the eternally crowded Streatham High Street near the cinema. When the lights changed and the traffic stopped several people crossed the road in both directions. I started to make my way without noticing anyone in particular, when half way across a woman stopped beside me, putting her hand on my arm. I looked at her, not expecting anything really but vaguely wondered what she wanted. She looked at me, smiled, leaned closer and said quietly,

"Your hair is beautiful."

Oh my goodness, how cool is that? Traffic lights do not stay in the pedestrian's favour for long enough to exchange pleasantries with strangers on the way across. Anyone familiar with Streatham High Street knows that crossing that road is no picnic. Concentration is required. Just imagine it, with a crowd of people flowing in both directions, there is always a certain amount of necessary interweaving to make it to the other side unscathed anyway. How sweet of her to notice me, never mind think nice thoughts about me, let alone make the bold decision to share her thoughts with me. What joy. I am blessed.

*

A pleasant and not so brief interaction took place in a well-known health and beauty emporium in the wonderful Covent Garden. I was already having a lovely Friday which had begun well with my much loved regular Friday early morning meditation meeting. In the shop I was holding a bottle of unscented shampoo and another of unscented conditioner, which I had noticed on the shelf for the first time that day. I amused myself for a while, as I pondered the endless possibilities of fragrance and property blends which I could create with the huge collection of essential oils, already owned by me.

While I mused, a lady appeared in front of me and asked if I had used the products before. She stood before me a vision of beauty, quite a bit taller than me, slender in grey t-shirt and blue jeans. Her beautiful face with gorgeous clear skin was framed by her crop of thin braids. They were quite neat so perhaps recently done, the look suited her. She was not a member of staff, just another customer wanting to engage.

I told her that I have never seen the range before but was intrigued by the possibilities and how it could be fun adding my own blends. I thought she wanted to chat about the bottles and their contents, but no. She asked me what products I use for my own hair and I confessed that I have no particular brand choice. I generally use whatever is to hand, buying whatever appeals in the moment. She kindly told me that she thought my short natural hair looked beautiful and well looked after. Of course, I thanked her, I was an ever grateful receiver of her kind comments.

It turned out that her reason for approaching me in the first instance was because she wanted to talk about my life with short hair. How did I find it? How did I look after it? What was the reaction from other people? What did men think? What did women think? What did I think? Well, that opened the flood gates and allowed a torrent of opinions, observations and examples to flow out.

She had grown tired of having her hair braided and while part of her really wanted to experience the freedom of natural hair, another part of her was really afraid of what she considered to be a drastic decision. Was she kidding me? Of course she should try it. There was nothing, absolutely nothing to be afraid of. I could only think of positives and besides, if she wanted to she could always choose to grow it again or go back to braiding or whatever she fancied. For goodness sake, cutting it is not the end of the world, it always grows again anyway. Then again, that was easy for me to say because I was already happily living with my hair short and unaltered.

She asked me if I had tried other hair styles. Well that was also another wonderful welcome opportunity for me to launch into some of my personal coiffing history. As a little girl with a West Indian mother, I was subjected from a tender age to the common and regular hair alteration process. The hot combs were no fun at all and I still remember my neck, ears and forehead being scorched by hot metal, while I sat through sessions accompanied by the smell of my burning hair.

I grew up always messing with my hair like so many black women. The repeated chemical application, perming, braiding and weaving were all part of everyday life. It all cost so much and it all took so long and what was the point? My hair was thick and strong and I was raised to believe that these were undesirable properties, so went along with the notion that being at the mercy of hairdressers was the way life should be. I never questioned it. However I did wonder why I was regularly paying fortunes to sit at the hairdressers for eight to twelve hours at a time, for hair that would look good for less than a week. Good grief, less than a week! I ask you, why, what was the point? The recommendation was to wait for three months before the next perm, so even with my maths, that is a lot of bad hair days.

I blundered my way through different hair effects, in an effort to find something that suited my lifestyle. I wanted to look pretty. I wanted to feel beautiful. I wanted to feel attractive. For my entire life I had never felt able to associate myself with any of those words. The whole weaving experience was like something out of a blockbuster comedy. I wanted hair that floated. I wanted to be able to flick it like a heroine from a romantic movie. I handed over great sums of money, sat in the chair morning 'til night and left with hair that did not suit me one bit. I felt compelled to leave it because of the financial and physical effort I had gone to in order to have it done. As for the braids they hurt, gave me a headache and temporarily damaged my hair line.

Then there was the whole black-women-can't-swim-because-of-their-hair thing. I could not swim and my hair was a huge factor. I had two small children and I wanted them to be able to swim. I did not want my hair to interfere with their ability to learn and I knew that children who swam well had a mother who took them swimming and took them often. A decision had to be made, enough was enough. On Friday 8th August 1997 I took myself to a hairdressers in Hammersmith and gave them the "there's no turning back, cut it all off" instruction. I remember the date because it was a momentous occasion and by that time I did not care whether it suited me or not. I had heard conversations about bone structure, jaw line, head shape, sexual preference, aggressiveness, political alliance, all manner of perspectives and perceptions, when talking about black women with short natural hair. I was none the wiser and had joined in with some of these non-evidence based discussions, which all went a long way towards delaying my decision to leave the hair perming/weaving/braiding brigade. Anyway, by decision day I no longer had any interest in what anyone thought or might choose to think about me or my personality. Something had to be done and I had to do it.

The hair was cut. I looked in the mirror and liked it. I loved it. I have loved it ever since. It was like having a ball and chain removed. I had not even realised it but for all of those years I was imprisoned by my hair. Suddenly I was free, free, I tell you, free.

Hopefully, all of this goes some way to explaining why compliments about my hair are a big deal, a big deal in deed. What about the three and a half years when I shaved my head and lived bald? Not much to say about it really. I had a lot of thinking to do and the intensely empowering experience of being bald helped me to learn about myself. Years later when I mentioned this period of my life to someone they asked what I was hiding from and my recollection is that I was not consciously hiding from anything because I did not feel anything but emotional numbness.

Just for the record, on the swimming front, my son had lessons, my daughter had lessons and I had lessons. I took them swimming two or three times a week and they are excellent swimmers. I took myself to a variety of pools even more often, morning, afternoon or evening to practise, practise, practise. I went from not being able to swim a stroke to swimming a thousand metres without stopping. Now that's a result.

Wow, after all that, time to return to the lovely lady in the shop. I obviously did not tell her all of that in quite so many words but I covered most of it. By the end of the conversation she said that she had really enjoyed talking to me, felt much better about everything and felt inspired to 'just do it'. I could not ask for more.

About three weeks later I was in a Central London library when I heard someone speak to me,

"Hallo, you probably don't remember me but we talked about hair a few weeks ago." There she was again, the lovely lady from the unscented shampoo shop. I was so glad she spoke to me, she thanked me again for helping her make a decision about her braids and assured me that when they grew out she was going to have them removed and 'go natural'. Frankly, it is no odds to me whether she braids or does not braid, whether she goes natural or does not go natural, so long as she is happy.

*

Amusing moments have involved my hair like the time I boarded a bus and passed a man sitting in the luggage shelf. Okay the bus was full and I stood with others and thought it a little quirky that the guy in front of me had chosen to sit on the shelf. He seemed happy enough and I saw no reason not to smile at him when he smiled at me. He said,

"I like your hair." How sweet of him, he continued, "You can't see mine," then he took off his hat so that I could see him better, again, how sweet. He scraped his fingers over his head a few times then laughed and said, "There isn't much of it but never mind."

That was the end of it, the bus got busier and I moved down towards the back.

*

I once had the pleasure of meeting a delightful lady who worked in a shop in Covent Garden. I was instantly attracted by the vibrant colour of her orange and red hair, like the sun shining inside the building. Wow, it was gorgeous so of course I had to tell her. After graciously accepting my compliment she said that she liked mine too. Oh yes, there was I forgetting how different and noticeable my own hair is. I sincerely hoped that she did not think I commented on hers so that she would notice mine. Silly me, why would such a daft thought cross my mind? My thoughts and verbal expressions were sincere and there was every reason to believe that hers were too. Then she said something which I had never been told before but has been mentioned since,

"Your silver hair creates a light around your face making your complexion glow, it looks like a halo."

Well, there is an image I could happily get used to, what a lovely thing for her to say, I was chuffed to bits. Over the next few months, I popped into the shop several times and enjoyed lively chit chat with the same lady often revolving around her selection of hair styles. One day it would be playful in two plaits, Heidi style, another day scraped back in a neat, elegant bun, another day loose, another day decorated with a flower, always something different, always a reflection of the mood in which she had woken up. My hair offers no such amusement, apart from growing a centimetre or two, then being cut, it is just about the same every day. When I pointed this out to her during one of our many lively enjoyable conversations she observed that this is probably the reason that I have a selection of hats.

How clever of her to notice and she had made a good point. Now then, if I have discovered that my hair is an excuse for people to talk to me, it has to be said that my hats seem to have a similar effect. Oh the fun I have and the fun they cause.

*

It was a winter's day, a Sunday and jolly cold. Well, why else would I be wearing my huge fur hat which is just the most exquisite item of head gear ever made. I owned it for a couple of years before I had the nerve to wear it. I must have been feeling pretty good when I bought it but could never pluck up the courage to go out in it. Never mind, I learned more about myself over time. I became comfortable with who I am, realised my power, cared less and less about the approval of others and last winter wore it lots and lots. It is black fur, round, deep and divine, oh by the way it cost a fortune.

I was in the queue for the café in the Royal Festival Hall of London's South Bank when a lady stood beside me, made eye contact and smiled before telling me that she liked my hat. It was very kind of her to say so and I said something I have said many times when strangers have commented on my lovely hat,

"Thank you, it's nice and cosy under here."

As we were waiting, I decided to share some information with her. I said that as it had been so cold recently I had taken to wearing my scarf underneath the hat to keep my ears warm. She expressed surprise and told me that she thought the two items were one unit. So I took them off to show her the combo and she loved the idea. What a lovely way to pass the time, while waiting for a cup of tea.

Then there was the time I wore another beautiful hat, this one pretends to be a knitted, woollen, cable number but is seriously jazzed up by the grey and black fur trim. I love it. The fur is long and tickles my face but it has the added bonus of giving me a chance to pretend I have fringe. Someone suggested that I 'give it a trim' but I told them they had missed the point of it entirely. On a day in early December I wore this hat on a bus when a woman behind me leant forward to tell me that she liked my hat. She seemed to think nothing of stroking it while she spoke to me. When I thanked her for the compliment, she moved in closer and said,

"You look very pretty under there."

How sweet of her to say so. She continued to stroke and asked if it was made of fox fur. Well it never occurred to me for a moment that anyone might think it was made of real fur never mind fox. Clearly I had much to learn.

Later the same day I visited a shop in Battersea where I have enjoyed friendly banter with one of the assistants on a couple of occasions. Both times I had found her to be incredibly chatty with a wonderful upbeat outlook on life, I liked her straight away and we conversed easily. Somehow during our first meeting we found ourselves comparing foreign travel stories, the joy of first class flights and the benefits of maintaining a positive perspective. The second time we met, she was just as talkative and she showed me a piece of fluffy fabric which she was intending to fashion into a hand warmer for the winter. I warned her to be ready for random strangers to stroke her in the street. Someone else overheard us and said that she would hate it if that happened and I told them I am used to it.

So there I was in the shop once again and as I walked in she greeted me with a friendly welcome. As I responded, I saw a handsome, young, well groomed, neat, slim chap standing beside her and I said,

"Hi there and who is this gorgeous man with you today?"

As soon as I had said it I wondered if I had taken a step too far but I need not have concerned myself. He beamed, introduced himself and quickly added,

"I'm always here on a Wednesday, perhaps you haven't been here on this day of the week, that's why you haven't seen me before." He continued brightly, "If you come here on a Wednesday you get both of us and I'm worth it aren't I?"

So no problem with his confidence then, I liked him already. I laughed and said to the lady,

"Well, I didn't need to ask you who this gorgeous man is because he knows he's gorgeous already."

He turned to serve another customer and I overheard him telling her about his new hat. I told them about the lady on the bus that same morning who asked if my hat was made of fox, expecting them to find it laughable. I was wrong. It transpired that the guy owns a gilet made of fox fur and a hat made of rabbit fur. So what do I know? Not much about the world of fur clothing it seems.

*

People stop me and talk about hats, people stop me and talk about hair and I have met strangers when the subject of French plaits has been the catalyst. There was the delightful lady from Stuttgart who I met in the breakfast queue on my tango holiday in Ireland. I described the joyful interaction in detail in my previous book and it was truly a special time.

Then there was the day I found myself plaiting the hair of a colleague while at work. The shop was quiet and we were happily passing the time. She liked her hair in a plait and I liked playing with her hair, so all was well. While I was busy creating one of my masterpieces, I became vaguely aware of a woman at the counter with her two children. As she turned to leave the shop she saw what I was doing and said,

"I could do with that."

Well, I had just finished and was idly pleasing myself by admiring my handiwork so I offered,

"That's okay, come and take a seat, I would be happy to plait your hair." I am not saying she looked surprised but she looked surprised. She said,

"Oh really, I couldn't." W ell, I was not going to force her and it is rarely an inclination of mine to insist but I simply, gently reiterated that if a plait was her wish then I would be happy to grant it.

"Oh that would be nice, thank you, how much is it?"

"No charge, see it as a gift." Okay, so she was surprised again but got over it and sat down. Her children seemed happy to stand quietly close by and wait patiently.

I took a moment to tune into her energy, well of course I did because that is what I do. Let us not ignore the fact that physical attention to the hair of another is also an emotional and spiritual experience, not to mention the issue of trust. Well it is, if we allow it to be. Moments before I began my triple woven creation she said,

"You don't remember me do you?"

Oh dear, oh dear, there was that question again to put me on the spot. I meet many people, so when I am presented with that question I speedily explore the recesses of my mind, the journeys, the careers, the schools, anywhere. If I remember them then whoopee, if not then there is no offence intended, it is about me not about them and I say, "Please remind me, where have we met?"

She said that we had spoken in the shop several months previously when she looked for something to help her six year old son who was experiencing digestive complications. My own path has clearly taught me about the undeniable link between physical health and emotional well-being. Whether we like it or not this applies to children as well as adults. She reminded me that at that time we talked briefly then I asked her if he was happy at school. Without hesitation, she told me that he never actually seemed to settle, about his unhappiness, his struggle with the children, the teachers, the work and at such a young age it was obviously not going well. He did not seem to enjoy school or want to go. Or course, changing schools was an option but could she be sure that life would be any better for him in another? I offered the perspective that regular schooling does not suit all children. I suggested home schooling, the benefits of meeting other families, supplementing subjects, working at his pace and the huge advantage of family holidays when you choose and not having 'the school run' to dominate your timetable.

Well that was months before and here she was again. So she remembered the conversation and it seemed obvious for me to ask,

"So ... how are things going?" She had taken him out of mainstream school and had been home schooling him for a few months. He had never been happier, had lots of new pals, and was thriving with advances in his core subjects which they had never thought possible. In addition, she had found a great network of other families so she was enjoying a wonderful new friendship circle. Her son was happier, she was happier, as a result, her husband was happier and they were planning to do the same with their younger daughter. She thanked me for my help that day and I thanked her for telling me about her family, I was delighted that all was well. I finished plaiting her hair. Did she like it? Of course she did, it looked lovely.

*

I love interactions with children, they are so open, so clear, so honest, particularly when they are allowed to follow their instincts. I remember being repeatedly told not to talk to strangers when I was a child and I was also frequently confused by the consequences when I did not answer when I was spoken to by someone I did not know. I tried to do as I was told but they could not have it both ways. No wonder I was scared to make up my own mind, whether to respond to an unknown adult or not. Now I am often surprised at how readily children seem to respond to me and I love it.

I remember one afternoon when I was sitting at my table ready to give hand massages if anyone fancied the experience. As usual, I had a selection of oils, creams and lotions and was happily enjoying my emotional and physical space. I noticed a woman at the other side of the shop paying for her items. Waiting patiently with her were a small child in a buggy and a little boy aged five as I found out later. I have no idea what prompted him but he left both is mother and sister and wandered over to my table. He was interested in the bottles and asked about the lotions. I told him what they were for and he asked to smell one. He was a bright young spark with huge brown eyes and fabulous crop of brown curly hair.

While he was busy enjoying the aromas his mother came over to join us. They both shared the same bright eyed joyous expression. I am quite aware that children often resemble their parents and they were a fine example. This delightful young man held out his hands and with his mother's permission I helped him to sample a couple of the unguents and rubbed his hands together. He seemed to enjoy smelling his hands and making appreciative noises and he offered his hands to his mother and little sister for both of them to smell.

He was an absolute treasure. Then he surprised me by naming the flowers depicted on the packaging. I was delighted to see him recognise rose, lavender and rosemary. His mother told me that he is fond of flowers and takes an interest in gardening. Well, I was impressed and fancied that I was in the company of a budding botanist or an aspiring aromatherapist. He was a joy to spend time with. This little boy returned his attention to the smells so we all went to the shelves of essential oils where he listened attentively while I told him a little about them. I was fascinated by his interest. He seemed more interested than some of the characters on my aromatherapy course, how funny.

All good things must come to an end and although we were having fun, they had other things on their 'to do' list. Before this fabulous family left my company, I put a couple of drops of essential oils on a folded paper towel for him to take away as a gift. He loved it, closing his eyes dreamily as he inhaled. I offered to write the names of the oils on the paper for him but he assured me that he would remember and his mother was confident that he would too. Such a wonderful mother and delightful children, they were happy, content and gave the impression of going with the flow. Chatting to them made my day and it was an honour to meet them.

*

Then there was the little boy in the bank with his father. The youngster spotted me and began a game of peek a boo as he hid behind his father's legs and poked his head from left to right and between the knees to smile and wave at me. Bless him.

Then there was the Sunday morning when I sat in the third floor gallery level of the Royal Festival Hall, yes I go there a lot. I was above the shop and enjoyed watching people passing below. Sometimes there are lots of people about but on this day I was pretty early so the other tables were free, where I had chosen to park myself. Down below was quiet, the shop had not opened yet and I glanced down to see two men walking and talking. Behind them trotted a small person, perhaps about two years old.

I have no idea what inspired him to look up but he did, spotted me and stopped. I briefly wondered what had captured his attention but there was no one else way up there, where I was, so I knew he was looking at me. He looked up, I smiled down at him and he smiled back. The two men had continued to stroll but the cute little person maintained his attention on me. I waved as I carried on smiling. His gaze was fixed and he seemed frozen in his tracks. One of the men, probably his father, turned around and seeing the young chap deep in concentration, walked back a few of paces to see what the distraction was all about. It was a moment of silence between me and the little boy but so much was communicated. The man called him but he did not respond. Unmoved, he continued to stare. I waved down at him again while the man walked back to him. Perhaps, he needed permission perhaps he did not but when his father said,

"You can wave back" he raised his little hand in the air towards me. His wave was a gift, so I said thank you. The three of them walked away together and the little boy turned waving repeatedly at me until they were out of sight. How cool it would be to know what was going through his young, fresh, keen mind, perhaps we will never know.

*

Then there was the time I travelled by train (a rarity for me) from Earlsfield to Waterloo. For some reason or another, the trains were packed Tokyo style, so I was squashed in with millions of other passengers with nothing to hold onto but equally with no fear of falling because I was wedged in by people on all sides. I had already decided to do my best to stay on the train at the end and let everyone else off, in an attempt to avoid being swept through the station by the mass populace.

As the train pulled in, I heard a man behind me issuing military style instructions to his family about staying together and waiting for the crowd to disappear before disembarking. I turned and laughed saying that he was doing just as I had planned to do. He seemed pleased that I approved and his group of adults all laughed along too while the three small children looked up, as if wondering what was going on.

His party and I were the last to leave the carriage. He returned to his logistics and directing his attention to the children, instructed them to "take an adult's hand". At that moment, a little boy looked up at me, I smiled and held out my hand. I did it in response to the army officer's instructions not expecting anything to happen but to my surprise, the little boy reached his hand up towards mine.

Oh how funny, he did not even know me, had never seen me before in his life but felt comfortable enough to hold my hand. His accompanying adults thought it was hilarious, we all laughed, they were a jolly bunch of people.

We wished each other a lovely day. To be honest I did not much fancy their chances at the Jubilee celebrations with the promise of rain and the strong probability of tired, hungry, fractious little people as the day progressed.

Media inspired events promoting excuses and opportunities for mass hysteria are not usually my thing, so why did I make the journey into town on such a day? I was on my way to a spiritual meeting in Covent Garden, which had been planned for months. The organiser did not cancel it, so neither did I. Was it worth it? Oh yes. Even the three hour walk home, in the rain from Chelsea, due to terminated public transport did not stop me having an outstanding experience. Yes it was definitely worth it.

That busy day reminds me of another such media inspired event, one Friday morning when I walked north along Shaftesbury Avenue towards one of my favourite cafés. As it turned out the café was closed, just about everything was closed, I later found a Starbucks open on the Charing Cross Road with about three people in it but apart from that not much was happening in commercial premises anywhere. However, out in the street, it was a very different story. There were people everywhere, excited people, excited flag waving people. For some reason they were all travelling in the opposite direction to me. Two of them humorously suggested that I turn around and someone else said I was going the wrong way but I just laughed because I had other plans.

A man on the other side of the road saw me, crossed over and walked with me, to tell me why he was not joining the masses to see the event. Perhaps I looked like I wanted to know. He had a few opinions to express about the monarchy, weddings, relationships and whatever. I did not really listen and I did not say much. There was no need really, he seemed happy to do the talking. I guess he picked me because I was the only person walking in that direction, so I suppose he thought I might be a kindred spirit. I had no view about the event either way and felt content enough to see the highlights on the television later if I felt so inclined.

*

I feel like returning to the events of the train for a moment. As the doors opened at Earlsfield, I was met by a wall of wedged people, I said, "Ah" and quickly walked to the next door hoping to find some improvement. It was not to be. It occurred to me that if I did not do something drastic, I was going nowhere. I stepped up, turned sideways and announced,

"Coming through!" It was not a question of someone making space for me, I could see there was nowhere for them to go. I created a groove with my advancing hip and shoulder and sliced my way through the bodies. I smiled and announced again,

"There, this is cosy isn't it?" Thankfully, a few people laughed, which was just as well because we were to be in close proximity for the duration. A couple got off at Vauxhall and a sweet little lady boarded. She looked petrified,

"Oh dear, I've got nothing to hold on to." I told her not to worry, gently pointing out that she had nowhere to fall anyway and she thanked me. I have no idea why but I felt the urge to mention that some nations travel like that every day, for their daily commute. She seemed impressed by my knowledge, asked questions about my travels, yes I have been to Tokyo on holiday, no, I have never actually lived there but squeezing on trains to work is a normal occurrence or so I am led to believe.

Carole Chandler

"Well, I suppose if I think about that I should think myself lucky," said my new friend the sweet little lady. I thought it was so lovely of her to continue with,

"You're so calm, I feel much better now."

So that is enough about trains and days of mass celebration. I return to encounters with small people.

*

I was just leaving a clothes shop on the Mitcham Road and as I passed a girl aged about eight years old, I heard her say in a loud voice,

"Hey! You weren't smiling just now." I turned to find her looking intensely at a child sized mannequin, which indeed had a kind of smirk on its face. The little girl was talking to it and she had made a declaration. I walked back and stood beside her, looking at the dummy. When the girl looked at me, I asked her if the face had changed and she insisted that it was not smiling when she passed it the first time. Interesting. I was in no position to confirm or deny her observation however, my broad view of life leads me to have no doubt that, she saw what she saw. If she said that the expression changed then who are we to say she was wrong? I congratulated her for noticing and left her to her observations.

*

One afternoon I walked along Tranmere Road in Earlsfield, as a mature couple left the front door of a house. On the pavement, they struggled with a plastic rain cover which they tried repeatedly to put on a stroller, much to the amusement of the occupant, a beautiful bonnie lass dressed in pink, chuckling away from her regal seating position. I was walking past, busy admiring the beauty and radiance of the child, when the grandfather looked up at me, smiled and spoke,

"I always as have trouble with these." Well he had my sympathy as I know they are far more complicated than they were when my children were small. Still, I was not planning to discuss equipment for long, as I felt compelled to smile at their beautiful baby and tell her so. She kicked her legs vigorously in response, the way that little people do when they are super bendy, with feet in the up beside the ear position. She chuckled and knew that what I was saying was true indeed. She really was very gorgeous. Grandpa was jolly and said to the baby,

"Did you hear that darling?" Oh yes, she heard it and she knew it. At just a few months old, she knew the truth when she heard it. I was about to walk on when the grandfather spoke again, "We are down here from Scotland for a week to help our daughter-in-law." How nice of him to tell me, how friendly of him to want to engage in conversation with me. I was flattered.

Carole Chandler

"Well, I'm sure your daughter-in-law is delighted and she is very lucky to have you." Between you and me, deep down in my heart of hearts I know it has nothing to do with luck but it felt like the right thing to say at the time, so I said it.

I had a different response from an adult when I complimented a baby in a café in London. The most gorgeous little girl, again a few months old sat in a high chair giggling as she watched me walk by. I sat at a table behind her and she turned to look at me. I love how young babies seem to turn their heads so far round, so easily, I often think they look just like owls. Her mother repeatedly called her with the offer of food but this little lady seemed intent on watching me. I laughed and she laughed, I waved and she bounced excitedly in her seat. I could not help myself but had to tell her that I thought she was beautiful, even though I am perfectly convinced that I was only confirming what she already knew.

Interestingly, mother was not impressed, she came out with,

"Oh dear, lots of people keep telling her that, I'm afraid she will get big-headed."

How would that even be possible? It says more about the mother than the baby. When did we stop celebrating beauty when we see it?

I was brought up in an environment where praising a child was not considered an option. The notion of creating big-headedness (whatever that means) was often cited as the excuse to withhold encouragement on any level. Thankfully, I know much better now. I have learned that when we see good in others, that is what we get. It works for all ages groups, I have seen evidence of this many times. Try it for yourself and see.

*

Then there was the evening I walked from my home along a quiet residential street and towards me came a lady pushing a cute little lad in a buggy. As I got closer I noticed that the mother had seen a cat and was trying to point it out to her little boy. Sadly for her she had competition because he had seen me and for some reason could not take his eyes off me. I heard her saying,

"Cat, cat, look there's a cat, not over there, over here, look, look!"

Yet, all he did was stare at me, me, stare at me, not over there, over here, stare stare. I heard her become increasingly irritated because she obviously really wanted him to see the cat and he seemed to not be taking any notice of her. She was totally unaware so I said,

"He didn't see the cat because he was too busy looking at me." She laughed without saying anything and carried on walking. This was fine because I waved at the young man as he disappeared down the road, still staring with the biggest, cutest smile on his face, this time craning his neck to look at me behind his buggy. How cool it would be to know what was going through this young, fresh, keen mind, perhaps we will never know.

*

Then there was the time I came out of a loo in a restaurant and passed a lady changing her baby's nappy. He was the cutest little chap with gorgeous, brown eyes and his toothless smile was enough to melt any heart. I was quite smitten by him as he grinned and the mother seemed surprised that he smiled at all. She said that the lady at the next table in the restaurant had been trying really hard to get a smile out of him but he would not oblige. Well he seemed to understand what she was saying because he just smiled at me even more. I said that perhaps the lady was trying too hard, perhaps we will never know but at that moment I was having fun.

The mother then went on to say that she was beginning to understand who he smiles at and who he does not respond to. That was wise of her to notice and I said,

"Babies know, they always know." That was the end of our meeting and once again I felt blessed.

*

Oh I had a wonderful, glorious, silent interaction with a small person a few months ago in Battersea Park. The whole experience had quite an effect on me. I was intending to buy some glass for my art in a shop close to home but when I spotted another glazier in Battersea High Street from the top deck of a number 44 bus, I followed the sudden urge to jump off at the next stop and walk back. I ordered a couple of pieces and the friendly man offered to prepare them straight away. All I had to do was give him half an hour.

I was happy to do that. I treated myself to a hot chocolate and a hot panini from a homely looking Italian café close by, then turned into a side street which led to the park. I was not sure where I was going but I knew the park was in that direction so assumed I would find somewhere nice to sit and enjoy my snack. This lovely open space is not a regular haunt for me, as I have not been there for over twenty years. It was a chilly day which gives me enough reason to wonder why I did not just stay in the café, as I am not usually one for sitting outside. Anyway, it was chilly and there was some distant activity in the park with groups of lads playing rugby in a field, another group of lads played some other ball based sport on a nearby court. I could not really see them, just heads bobbing up and down behind a fence. Apart from the occasional person walking a dog (or three), I had the place to myself. I was not intending to be there for long, as it was really much too cold for me to enjoy just sitting outside. From my bench I had view of a path perhaps about fifty metres to the right and a bit further ahead. Okay the measurements do not claim to be exact but you get the picture.

A little red figure appeared way down the path. Behind her, pushing a buggy, was a lady on her mobile phone. Neither of them seemed to be in any hurry. The little girl in her red snow suit toddled slowly ahead and I watched her. It did not occur to me for a moment that she would see me, I was sure that I was too far away. She was easily less than two years old and just toddling along as only a toddler can. She surprised me, she stopped, she did see me. She just stopped and stared. The lady, perhaps her mother, overtook her and carried on walking. For some reason, I had this delightful little lady's attention. I waved. She waved back. How could she even see me? I have no idea and I did not really care, I enjoyed watching her too, I idly wondering why she felt so compelled to stop and why she felt the impulse to gaze.

Children are always so interesting, the younger they are the more they follow their own guidance. The younger they are, the less they are negatively influenced by the circumstances and events which surround them. The younger they are, the more they remember who they are. We could all learn from them. I know that I have.

There is something magical about remembering how to see the world through the eyes of a child. To learn to engage with our inner child is a gift we can give ourselves, remembering how to be playful again and have fun. That is what life is about after all. In the words of a beautiful song by the great George Benson, *'let the children's laughter remind us how we used to be'*.

I rediscovered the playful side of my character a few years ago and now readily acknowledge that this is an important part of me to embrace. Some people do not feel comfortable with my fun side but I am no longer willing to suppress it, in order to feed the insecurity of others, so there. I have learned about my connection and this is something which babies and small children instinctively maintain until they forget, as they get older, it is drummed out of them by people who have also forgotten. Never mind, I do not need to worry about that any more or ever again. I understand how the world works now, I know and understand that each little person has things to teach and they have things to learn. We all do. Life is good and all is well.

So there was this little cutie watching me and there I was watching her. I waved again and her teeny arm waved back. She continued to watch me. A few paces ahead the mother was off the phone and looking back. She saw me wave and unaware that the baby had already responded, the lady called out,

"Go on, wave, you can wave if you like." Well I was grateful to her for allowing her baby to wave at a stranger, not that the little girl needed her permission because she had already made her instinctive decision to wave. I was treated to another wonderful wave and it felt fantastic. Such a gift just for me, I was blessed. Following repeated encouragement to proceed, the little person walked on but not without looking back and waving several times, as they progressed along the path. Like I said, the whole experience had quite an effect on me. I have an abundance of experiences of babies and children waving at me and engaging with me in some way or another, so I have no idea why I was particularly touched by this one. I just know that I was. How cool it would be know what was going through this young, fresh, keen mind, perhaps we will never know.

*

Then there was the time I went to the ladies in the huge enormous Marks and Spencers in Merton High Street. The door opened just as I arrived, out came an elderly lady and behind her strolled two little girls. They were just the cutest little girls ever. When they saw me, they both stopped in their tracks and stared up at me. They looked up and I looked down. Their bright eyes seemed to really be concentrating on me, so I said,

"Hallo ladies, are you having fun today?" The door was being held open by the old lady who called them, as they slowly shuffled towards her, still staring at me. I looked at the lady who smiled in response to mine and I said they looked so cute. Both aged about three years old, one blonde with the biggest blue eyes ever and the other with dark brown hair and the biggest brown eyes ever. They seemed reluctant to leave the doorway or take their eyes off me, which was fine as I was quite happy to enjoy their cuteness.

I said, "You are both very beautiful aren't you?" The brown eyed cutie giggled for some reason. Little Miss Blue Eyes said,

"What are you called?" I loved her question, not what is your name but what are you called. Well, I am called all sorts of things but I concluded that this was probably not the arena to complicate matters, so I simply said,

"My name is Carole." At that moment the gorgeous, little, sweet, brown haired cherub raised both of her arms and reached her hands up towards my face. With no words, no smile, no change of expression, she just stretched up, so I bent down, held out my hands, she touched my face then put her hands in mine. The lady said nothing while all of this was going on until she invited them to say goodbye.

I said, "Goodbye angels, have a lovely day." They retreated sideways, continuing to watch me and wave to me, until they disappeared through another set of doors.

It was all very interesting and I do not really know what happened that day but these two little sweethearts crossed my path for some reason and meeting them was a magical moment.

*

Then there was the day I heard a baby crying in a restaurant. Babies cry and that is okay, most of the time I take no notice, it just depends. This little one, a few weeks old, was not just having a moan, he seemed pretty angry about something, so I found myself paying attention. His mother tried a few things to console him. She put him in his pram, still shouting and complaining, then she changed her mind and picked him up again, still shouting and complaining, bless him and bless her. A baby crying is none of my business, unless I choose to make it so. On that occasion something inspired me to leave my table and walk over to the shouting baby and the slightly flustered mother. I looked at her, smiled, paused and softly asked,

"What does he want?" She had no reason to answer me, she was entitled to tell me to mind my own business, my intrusion was unrequested and had she objected I would have completely understood. However, my intentions were sincere and from the heart, which I suppose is what she responded to.

"He wants the breast but I'm not going to let him."

"You don't want to feed him?"

"I fed him half an hour ago for about an hour."

"Well, he is definitely not hungry then." I spoke with confidence from my experience of helping hundreds of breast feeding mothers during years of work with newborns. Breast feeding is really not the mystery it is made out to be and I felt that confirming what she already knew might be appropriate for her, just in case doubt was creeping in about whether to feed him again or not. I felt inspired to ask another question,

"Is his tummy alright because he is arching his back?"

"Do you think he has wind?"

"Possibly. Have you tried holding him like this?" I said as I demonstrated with an imaginary baby in my arms. She looked confused, I gestured again but she did not know what I meant, so I stretched out my hands towards her and said,

"May I?" She handed me her baby. I repeat, she handed me her baby. I fully understand that this is a massive compliment. She handed me her baby. I am quite aware of the honour that she paid me by trusting me implicitly and I appreciate that. I held him the way I had described, put my hand on his back and he stopped shouting. She said, "Well that's a new one."

Her young man realised something was going on and was quiet, until he lost interest in the new activity and started to whimper again but with nothing like his previous noise level. He seemed more irritated than angry by this point. I turned him and suggested she put her finger in his mouth, which she did and he was happy. A young baby, no matter how young will not be placated by a finger if he is genuinely hungry. He was happy, mother was happy, my work was done, I wished her a peaceful day and returned to my meal. She left with a quiet baby and hopefully feeling a little less drained.

*

Then there was the day I sat in a lovely café, happy in my own space just enjoying myself, writing lists of things that I appreciate about my life, watching people come and go, chatting occasionally to the staff who know me well, as I go there often. A beautiful lady came in with a teeny baby in a papoose and in a buggy sat a wise old man in a toddler's body. From the moment she arrived, her passenger on wheels saw the opportunity to call out his preferences. First it was,

"Water, water, water, I like water." When mother acknowledged his request he raised his game to,

"Pasta, pasta, mummy pasta pasta, I like pasta." He was simply adorable, persistent and adorable. I had a clear view of him from my seat, so when I smiled at him, I was delighted to receive his gorgeous cute smile in return. Interestingly, when a chap at another table tried to engage with this sweet little boy, he chose to hide behind his rain hood. I am quite sure he had his reasons.

As if by way of confirmation, the "pasta pasta I like pasta" song continued. It was hilarious for me, perhaps not quite so much fun for his delightful and patient mother, who tried to order at the counter while satisfying his need to be heard and answered. She did a very good job from where I was sitting, especially as I have witnessed parental intolerance in the face of less that this young man's continual 'love of pasta' declaration. I looked from him to her and said quietly,

"I think he likes pasta", she smiled and said, "Yes, he always wants pasta."

It is so nice to know that children really know what they want. How interesting that this simple fact is frequently ignored and adults assume they know better. Surely in the arena of food preference, we all know the tastes we like, don't we? I mean how something tastes, is a personal thing, is it not?

A few months ago, I heard a woman in the shop talking about her seven year old son, who declined her kind offer of certain foods because he knew what he preferred. She was convinced that being autistic, he seemed to have an associated inability to decide for himself. This mother joked about buying a milk alternative which she knew he did not like, with the intention of decanting it into the packaging of his favourite, to 'fool' him. Autistic or not, label or not, no child is a fool. They know more than they are given credit for. Perhaps my best course of action would have been to reduce my risk of becoming outraged by the injustice, to mind my own business, to walk away and find something to think about that felt better. Instead I said, somewhat boldly,

"He may be autistic but he's not stupid, he will know it is not the same and he won't thank you for it." The laughter stopped. The staff are used to me and my perspective on life. The lady looked at me and said quietly,

"Do you think I'm wrong then?" It was a simple question and one which I did not feel inclined to answer. I chose to keep any further thoughts to myself and remembered that she was doing what she thought was right at the time, with the information, knowledge and experience that she had. Her son equally was absolutely fine, so I did not need to be concerned about him either. I simply had to remember that there was nothing wrong really, she was perfect and he was perfect.

I removed myself from the situation and asked myself, why I was so bothered by something so unimportant. Well, I shall tell you why. When I was a little girl, I had food I did not like, mixed in with other food, in an attempt to 'fool' me. I always knew. For me it was not just a matter of taste, it actually induced nausea and vomiting. In my strict environment, complaining was not acceptable, spitting it out was not an option and vomiting led to unpleasant consequences. I was caught between the proverbial rock and hard place. Some adults are uncomfortable with children expressing themselves and by their pure size can temporarily induce submission from a small person. I learned to reduce myself for self-preservation. Believe me, memories like those make me forget who I am and lead me to plead the case for children being given food they do not like. Clearly there is emotional work for me to do in that area, I shall just pop it on my list and attend to it later.

That is quite enough now Carole, breathe, breathe, breathe.

*

So back to the pasta loving mini man, who sat beautifully with his mother and baby for a short while before requesting a visit to the loo. All three of them set off and as she passed one of the café staff, she responded to a question by saying that one of her children was just a few weeks old and the other nearly two, also adding that life is hard work with them both. I felt for her, mothering small children is exhausting. They returned and sat peacefully together at a table on the far side of the café and I was hardly aware of them, until I decided to leave.

With my coat on and bag in hand, I passed their table on my way out. The little lad, bounced on his seat, smiled at me and laughed a cute infectious little laugh. I made eye contact with the mother who looked bright and radiant too with her braided hair, clear smooth skin, lovely brown eyes and her small baby content in her arms. It truly was a peaceful setting to behold. I followed the urge to say,

"You really are a lovely lady with your two beautiful children."

"Oh thank you but it's really hard work." Well I felt for her again. Her children were adorable, with her lively toddler and resting baby, she gave the impression of a mother who was coping admirably with her young brood but clearly the demands were bothering her. I offered an opinion, from my heart, from my place of love, I spoke as I felt guided,

"Yes, you're right, it is hard work being a mother with two small children." Then without knowing anything about her lifestyle, interests, schedule or commitments I felt inspired to continue, "You'll find life much easier if you go at their pace more."

She seemed interested and asked me what I meant. I said a few things about life before babies compared to life after babies and the exhaustion which ensues when trying to combine the two. While it is possible, it is not sustainable, something has to give. She said,

"Yes, you're right, I know you're right." When I have had this conversation with other mothers, like her they have agreed. She asked for suggestions, I was happy to oblige, after a few, she thanked me. I have discovered that some mothers welcome permission to change pace, to do what feels instinctively right and slow down.

By way of example I am reminded of a time a couple of months ago, one weekday afternoon, when I was walking down a road perpendicular to Garratt Lane not far from Earlsfield station. About half way down the road, I approached the entrance to a church hall, when just ahead of me I heard the most almighty rumpus. A lady carried a wee little infant, so wee and so little one could have been forgiven for thinking he was only a few hours old. Of course that is ridiculous so let us assume that he was a newish newborn. Behind her was a girl aged about three wearing a pink leotard, pink ballet skirt, tights and pink ballet slippers. How one so small can make a noise so loud is always a source of amusement to me. This little ballerina shouted and screamed and yelled and was clearly seriously displeased about something. With all of the commotion they were going nowhere in a hurry, so I managed to catch up with them. I stopped and said to the mother,

"Is this before or after ballet class?" She sighed and told me that they had just arrived for the class but her daughter had complained and cried all the way there and refused to go in, yet was still crying even though they were going home. Oh dear, poor woman, I felt for her but I felt for the little one too, as she was distressed. When I asked if she usually likes ballet, mother said that she went a couple of times but announced, that day before leaving, that she did not want to go again. Mum had just bought the 'uniform', as she called it, so insisted that they go.

Ouch, that's a lot of trouble to go to with a tiny baby and a reluctant young lady. I asked if it was worth it, mum confessed that she wished she had not bothered.

"You won't do that again will you?"

"No I won't, definitely not."

"They always know what they want and sometimes it's easier to just be guided by them." I was on a roll so I added, "I know it can be really annoying when they change their minds about doing something but it won't be the last time."

This all took me back to my early days with a little ballerina who also made a sudden unexplained decision to never go again after less than a term. I never doubted her decision to stop, children know what they want. I also had a young musician who at one stage or another had his own, violin, guitar, 'cello, saxophone and piano and did really well with private lessons and examinations, yet dropped them all at a moment's notice. I never doubted his decisions to stop, children know what they want.

It is not my job to override their inner guidance. I must have tuned into that on some level even before I became consciously aware of the lessons I have learned about the importance of trusting my gut instincts.

I am also reminded of the time I witnessed a mother in our shop with a little toddler who made it quite clear that he did not want to be in his buggy. Squirming and complaining he wriggled and writhed his way out of his harness, climbed out of his pram and walked around a bit. He enjoyed a brief moment of freedom until his mother discovered his escape and attempted to reinsert him into his place of incarceration, or so it would seem given his objections in the moment.

He shouted and shouted and arched his back and I could not help laughing even though I tried not to. Luckily the mother could not see me as she fought to put him back. I laughed because the episode reminded me of my son at eighteen months old who had a way of preventing me from putting him in his buggy too. I could never work out how my baby could have the strength to prevent me, an adult, from picking him up and placing him in his buggy and walking away. How indeed. However, astonishingly (well I was astonished anyway) he would arch his back, hold himself rigid, making it virtually impossible for me to pick him up. Other times I might be already holding him when he went into body-rigid-back-arched mode, then he would be impossible to manoeuvre. Whenever this happened, I would have no choice other than to ride it out, wait for him to run out of steam and return to a limp more manageable, more moveable bodily condition.

In retrospect I probably did little to alleviate the situation because whenever he trumped me with his 'I'm not getting in' power, I would practically collapse with laughter. Sometimes I could hardly control myself but I always found it funny. What kind of I'm-the-parent-and-I'm-in-charge message was I giving? It was too late to worry about that when I was doubled over by the hilarity and absurdity of the situation, I mean really, he was just a baby. How was it even possible that I could not put him where I wanted him to be? It just goes to show.

So there I was in the shop trying my hardest not to openly laugh at the woman with her little back archer. Maybe it is a boy thing because my daughter never did it, then again they are quite different personalities. I wandered over to console the mother and opened with,

"You poor thing, my son used to do that when he was about the same age."

She was obviously not finding it funny, continued to battle with him and responded sternly,

"Well, mummy always wins." Well if this was a win or lose situation I did not really fancy her chances. Her son may have been little but he did not look like a quitter. I was intrigued by her perspective and asked,

"You always win do you?"

"Oh yes I do. Well, when it matters anyway." She said it with such determination. I briefly wondered if this was an, 'it matters' situation but I did not care enough to ask, so wished her luck and walked away.

Anyway, time to take my attention back to the pasta-pasta-I-like-pasta person. His mother agreed that slowing down was a desirable option yet wondered if it was possible. I said that it may feel like giving in but it is really not. You feel so much better, life is so much easier, you have more energy and have more chance of enjoying your children. She laughed and I laughed and it felt like a useful exchange of ideas. She heard me and was thankful.

Then her young man stood on his seat and announced that he wanted to visit the loo again. Well, I could have easily left them all to it, I knew she was infinitely capable and did not need any interference from a stranger but I could also see that she had her hands full with the younger person. Besides, she had done the bathroom trip not long before with both of them and declared it to be 'a right performance' on their return. To be honest, I did not really think about it, I just blurted it out,

"Will he let me take him?" I half expected her to say thanks but no thanks and half expected him to insist on mummy. I did not mind either way. All I did was offer, with no emotional attachment to the response. She said,

Carole Chandler

"Oh I don't know if he will," looked at him and said, "will you?" At that moment he started to climb over her to leave the table. She laughed and moved her legs out of the way so he could climb down more easily and he announced,

"Yes, I go with the lady." Ooh, such a confident little man, he did not even look back. I asked him if he knew the way and assuring me he did, said

"I show you, I show you." I followed him up the stairs, which must have been like climbing a mountain for his little legs. He opened the doors himself, managing very well, told me to wait for him, talked non-stop, loved the soap bottles and screamed his disapproval of the automatic hand dryer, shouting, "Ahh! Too loud! Too loud!"

That was a useful lesson for me and one worth remembering if I should ever find myself in a similar situation again, before silent hot air hand driers are invented. On the way back down the stairs he sweetly told me that he loves his baby brother, we were back in the restaurant and he ran to his mother and lil' bro'.

What can I say? I was honoured to be accepted by this delightful young man and his equally delightful mother. They did not know me, I did not know them, we had met only moments before. So much trust in such a short space of time. It was another blessed moment of magic and I have no words to adequately describe the joy I felt.

*

Then there was the time a couple of years ago when I passed a cute little boy sitting in the baby seat of a supermarket trolley, in a store in Richmond. I had not really noticed him until he leaned over the side stretching out his arm to touch me as I walked by. I stopped and said,

"Hi there, you want to say hallo to me do you? How nice." I held out my hand and he grabbed my fingers. It is always fun to be reminded how strong babies are. The lady pushing the trolley turned out to be his grandmother and she expressed surprise at her nine month old grandson's behaviour because as she said,

"He never normally takes to strangers." Well, what could I say? Perhaps he did not see me as a stranger. Perhaps we had met before. I decided to keep my conjecture to myself. Having just met, I hardly knew her well enough to have that level of discourse.

She may have been surprised but I was not nearly so much. I have heard it before. A lady came into the shop one morning with a young man in a stroller. I had a little silent play with her toddler as he hid behind his hood and I hid behind my fingers and he turned his head away and I turned my head the other way and he looked back to see if I was still there and I looked surprised and he laughed and I laughed and we both had fun. His mother said with a hint of a grunt,

Carole Chandler

"You're lucky, he doesn't usually talk to strangers and he's normally grumpy in the mornings", to which I said,

"Well, he's not grumpy now, we're having fun, your lovely cute son is playing with me."

This was all reminiscent of the morning I turned off Garratt Lane towards the Blackshaw Road and passed a woman pushing a buggy with a little boy passenger and ahead of them, her little girl in school uniform was riding a scooter. Mother looked a little fed up to say the least but for all I know she was having a good day from her perspective, so I let her be. Meanwhile, the buggy boy saw me and smiled, waved his arms, pointed at his sister and babbled something which I could not make out. I said,

"You're a chatty young man aren't you, is that your sister?" He chuckled and babbled some more, I was still none the wiser but he seemed to be having fun. I smiled at his mother who chose not to smile back and I said,

"He seems to be a happy little boy." Just like the other mother she said,

"You're lucky, he's normally grumpy in the morning."

*

There was the time I went into a grocers type newsagents in Mortlake. On the counter sat a baby, a small baby, just a few months old, with her father standing beside her at the other side of the counter. Well, most people like babies and this little girl would have captured the heart of anyone I suspect. With possibly the largest, brightest brown eyes I have ever seen and a mass of dark brown curly hair, she had my attention. I could not help myself,

"Hallo there, you're beautiful aren't you?" I distinctly remember offering my hand but the occasion was a few years ago when I was far less sure of myself, so I did not stretch out my arm or reach towards her. I was still not confident enough to do that in case it upset her. The last thing I wanted was a negative response. I had been at the receiving end of quite enough of those over the years, thank you very much.

I raised my hand and watched her move from the far side of the counter, away from her father's arms, she turned herself onto her hands and knees and crawled towards me. I can remember it now like it was yesterday. What a compliment. What an honour. I had been accepted. I had been accepted by a baby. There was no judgement, I was okay, I was a good person after all. Yay!

Not bad eh? Not bad coming from a person who was told years ago that she frightened babies. Surely not, surely I mistaken, perhaps I misunderstood. Well, picture the scene, I visited a work friend who was on maternity leave, her partner was holding their precious new baby when I looked at him, said hallo and the baby cried. The daddy said,

"Don't look at him, your face is too animated, you're frightening him."

What the hell? How that comment haunted me for years. I was already someone utterly convinced that I was unworthy, unlovable and without value. All he did was feed my insecurities. Thankfully, I have since learned the truth. I am highly unlikely to receive a remark like that now but if I did I would know exactly what to do with it.

Well, let me give you an example. I was at lunch about a year ago with a friend from the past, someone who I had not seen for a couple of years but who I had spent a lot of time with during my former years of low self-esteem and low self-worth and low, well, everything really. Unfortunately for him, he thought he was engaging with the old me but I was different. I was learning how to allow myself to be me, the greatest gift that I could give myself.

It was lovely to see him again as I had always enjoyed his company and he had been a great source of comfort to me during some troubled times. Anyway, I mention this because speaking my truth in his company was a milestone for me. He was a friend, an old friend, so not technically a stranger but he might as well have been, as he did not really know me anymore. I am positive that our friendship may have survived but he said things which he was used to saying, yet did not resonate anymore and he displayed more than one personality trait which did not sit well with me anymore either. I am no longer the insecure person he used to know. I no longer accept the unacceptable, so it felt better to let him go, saying that there will always be space for him in my heart, I wished him well and I have not seen him since.

My counsellor wisely told me years ago, that a certain amount of friendship pruning would be necessary as I transitioned from the old me to the real me. It turned out that this chap was the last casualty in the pruning process. It feels like losing people and is one of the hardest aspects to deal with when we move from disempowerment to regaining our power again. From that familiar place of disempowerment, family and friends are accustomed to treating you in an established pattern. They know you will tolerate thoughts, words and actions of which you do not approve but you lack the strength or knowledge to complain. Often from a place of acknowledging unacceptable behaviour you allow them to continue unchallenged.

An early lesson was to learn how to say no. I am eternally grateful to Oprah Winfrey for her show many years ago on this very subject. I suppose I would have eventually learned to stop being an undervalued, unappreciated, taken for granted door mat, without her show but that discussion kick started me perfectly, at a time when it was precisely what I needed. I watched and learned, my new skill was put into practise immediately and it was such a big deal that I remember the person who received my first conscious, refusal. It was my first, this-is-not-what-I-want-so-I-am-not-going-to-do-it, NO!

Once I learned that my thoughts about myself were the first point of change, I was well on my way to recovery.

Ouch, suddenly I was fighting back.

Ouch, suddenly I was no longer accepting the unacceptable.

Ouch, suddenly I was not tolerating the intolerable.

Some people did not like that. Some of them disappeared. A lot of them disappeared. In metaphysical terms, they vibrated their way out of my experience.

It felt like starting again on the friendship ladder but I had to ask myself, which did I prefer, lots of people expecting the old me or a select few positively loving, knowing, nurturing and understanding the new me, the real me. I know which feels better, I know which is more fulfilling and I know which is more life enhancing. My focus, my goal is self-appreciation as well as appreciation of others and that is all that matters.

This is what I share with many of my clients. This is part of my motivation to write my books, it is one of the aspects, which inspires me to share. I have clients who come to me instinctively knowing that personal changes need to be made, that their self-destruction is unwanted. What holds them back? Concerns about what their nearest and dearest might think. They have to stop caring about that, if they are to be joyful. They have to put their own feelings first. I had to stop caring about what other people think. I had to put my feelings first. Strangers never used to talk to me, now they do every day, everywhere. I used to wonder why, I don't any more.

Although the pruning process was inevitable, it left me in a bit of a friendship dessert. I had to trust that I would be fine. All I had to do was appreciate the present moment, visualise my positive future, pay no attention to the past and I just knew I would be fine. I learned the power of finding things to feel good about and remembering how I wanted things to be, so for a while, I pretended to have friends. This is where the 'Loose Women' show came in handy. They were my pals and I had fun with them on a regular basis, I loved them all but particularly paid attention when Carol McGiffin and Jane MacDonald were on the line up, their views really resonated with me. Thanks ladies you were a great comfort to me.

Something else helped me, I learned the power of laughter. Finding things to feel good about is one thing, finding things to laugh about is another. I watched comedy, a lot of comedy in a variety of forms, animation, movies and stand-up comedians. I enjoyed hours and hours of anything that made me laugh.

At first it took some effort, it can be hard to laugh at something when you do not feel so good. I practised, I laughed if something was funny, I laughed even if it was not. They say fake it until you make it and that worked for me. Pretending to laugh became a new skill to the point where I would forget that I was pretending, my sore ribs and watering eyes were funny enough reason to continue laughing. However, between you and me I had to give up on some of the stand-up guys, let's face it, a disproportionately high number of them are not in a good feeling emotional place and have the stage as their arena to complain about so much. Still, I am grateful to them, for it was good experience for me to see their performances and learn what I wanted.

En route to joy and fun, I discovered the fabulous Ellen DeGeneres who reigns supreme. The cost of satellite TV was worth every penny to have access to her, genuinely funny, ever adorable, childishly joyful, generously giving, enthusiastically playful and loving spirit. She is an amazing teacher and from her place of self-appreciation and self-awareness, she gives the distinct impression that she is living life from a happy, happy, happy, happy, happy perspective. I am eternally grateful for all I have learned from her about how to be myself.

So self-appreciation did not come easily, I had to learn and practise. After all, how could I expect others to value me if I did not know how to value myself? Once I discovered it was what I wanted, I devoted attention and effort to becoming the positive being that I was looking for in others. In the words of the great George Benson, *"Learning to love yourself, is the greatest love of all."* Now I let my light shine and allow the Universe to send me wonderful people and experiences.

*

So where was I? Ah yes, babies and small children. Well they interact with me every day and each one is a joyous moment. I shall share some of the many bus related experiences in my next book but for now I feel inspired to end my young people tales with a really delightful, I mean truly delightful occurrence from about a month ago. It was so sweet and special, that I make no apology for deciding to put it in both books.

I stood at the Wimbledon Road bus stop on Garratt Lane minding my own business, waiting for any of the four routes going to Tooting Broadway. A woman walked towards me and behind her shuffled a little boy, I'm guessing about two years old. She passed me and stopped to rummage for something in her bag. Meanwhile, her little chap stopped by my feet, looked up at my face, turned towards the road with his back towards me and ... (wait for it...) he leaned against my legs. Wow, come on, seriously folks, how relaxed and comfortable does a child need to be to lean against the legs of a stranger in the street? I mean, I ask you.

I am convinced that he was fully aware and knew precisely what he was doing. As for his mother, well I cannot speak for her. She turned, saw him chilled out in a semi recline against my pins and shrieked. She leapt forward, grabbed him by the front of his jacket and yanked him up into the air. Comically, his little legs dangled as she shouted at him,

"Stop it, don't do that!" I tried to say that it was okay, he was fine but she just said,

"I'm so sorry, I don't know what he's doing." Bless her poor lady, I would have preferred her not to be distressed but her reaction was out of my control. Bless them both.

*

Well now, babies and little people are a different species to teenagers. While the former are in tune with their inner knowing, the latter are often in the midst of negativity and doubt. They question frequently and receive unsatisfactory answers, hence the impulse to strive for individuality which leads to a variety of forms of expression. I understand where they are coming from, I have survived two teenagers of my own and fortunately I learned a while ago, the benefits of giving them less to push against, so life just became easier. They prefer to interact with their own age group, are often suspicious of the older generation and are fiercely protective of their personal space. All this said, I value any occasion when a young adult chooses to interact with me as a stranger.

It was a cold wintery evening, end of October, early November when I passed the parade of shops between Plough Lane and Garratt Lane. Neither of which is a lane in the true sense of the word, as they are both huge, wide, busy, high traffic routes. Anyway, the shops back onto a housing estate and occasionally, well often, one or two questionable individuals may emerge from the region. I am purposely deciding to be non-specific because as ever I aim to see people at their best.

On this particular evening it was not especially late but it was dark. I became vaguely aware of some activity behind a wall ahead of me, figures appearing, laughing, talking, retreating and intermittent banging sounds with evidence of orange, red and yellow sparks here and there. A woman come out of a shop and screamed. A man walked by and shouted. I chose to maintain my focus and assume that whatever was going on would have no impact on me.

I saw a few figures as I passed the wall, smiling to myself I let them be and all was quiet, no movement, no sound and certainly no sparks. A few paces on, the rumpus recommenced behind me. A little further along the road, a young lad, about fourteen years old crossed from the other side of the street and walked beside me. Even for me this was a little unusual, especially given his age and the teenagers' propensity to stay close to their own age group. I smiled at him as we continued walking and he opened the dialogue with,

"Do you like fireworks?" That was an interesting question. Did I wonder why he had chosen to ask me? Briefly but I decided to go with the flow and see what transpired.

"That depends where they are," I replied.

"My friends are down there by the shops trying to frighten people walking past."

"That's an interesting thing to do."

"What do you think about that, don't you think it's bad?"

"It doesn't really matter what I think, so long as you know what you think."

"Well, I don't want to get into trouble so I'm going home."

"So you've decided what is right for you, well done."

"Yeah, I'm getting far away before they hurt someone."

"Well done and good for you, I hope you are proud of yourself for making a sensible decision."

His big cheesy grin gave me the distinct impression that he was pretty pleased with himself and when we reached the corner of the road, he went one way and I went the other. It was quite an interesting interaction indeed.

*

Then there was the time I found myself walking down the Broadway in Wimbledon, I was singularly unimpressed to see a group of four lads standing kerbside, heckling a couple of albeit beautiful but seemingly uninterested teenage girls. Oh dear, to me it looked bad. To me it made a bad impression. To me it conveyed a poor message.

I did not really think about it and had not decided what I was planning to say but I called one of them over. I chose the loud one, the group speaker, the one who seemed to be the heckle leader. One of the other lads came with him, a third stayed a few paces away and the fourth hid in a doorway.

"I have a son a couple of years older than you and I like to think that I have taught him how to be respectful to women. What do you think your mother would say if she saw you shouting at girls in the street?" He looked down, thought about it but not for long because we both knew that he was fully aware of the answer. He confirmed that his mother would not like it at all.

"Also, if you really want young ladies to notice you and like you, then shouting at them in the street is not a good way to get their attention." To my surprise the other two joined us, so all four of them were in front of me, all standing close together, all looking at me. I said a few things about being charming, positive reactions, talking politely and sensible choices. They were actually listening. Perhaps I had taken a risk by stopping them but it did not feel like it at the time. My intention was not to chastise, I spoke to them with love from my heart. I like to think that they felt that, I like to think that they understood that and I think that is why I had their attention.

It would be an understatement to say that my own teenage son was unimpressed when I told him of the day's events.

"Oh no mummy you didn't!" Oh well, never mind, can't win 'em all.

*

Then there was the time I sat in the front passenger seat of a car parked by a kerb. A group of three tall lads were playing football on the pavement when the ball strayed and bounced on the bonnet of our vehicle. I opened the window much to the minor distress of the friend sitting beside me in the driver's seat, who made a small plea for me not to say anything. He had no reason to worry because I was not worried. I just had a word or two which I wished to share with the footballers.

With a slow deliberate 'come hither' of my index finger I beckoned the culprit. His friends left him to walk over to our car on his own. Within seconds I had said what I wanted to say, he apologised then walked away. My work was done.

The sigh of relief from my companion was audible. I have no idea why he was so worried, we had known each other for a long time, so he should have been used to me. Another time we walked together in north London where he had invited me to visit his new apartment. On the main road we saw an unusually high number of uniformed police and cars and their presence alarmed him. He expressed concern about possibly having bought a property in a problem area. I did not want him to be anxious, so the obvious thing to do seemed to be to ask the officers what they were up to. He was not impressed with my idea,

"Oh no Carole, please don't." It was too late as I was already smiling at an officer who seemed comfortable with me interrupting his day.

"Hallo, this is friend of mine and he has just bought a flat near here. We were just wondering why there are so many police here because he's worried that he's moving to a rough area now." The officer could not have been more accommodating. With a laugh he seemed happy enough to tell us that they were doing random checks for unlicensed cabs. He assured us that it is a relatively trouble free area and so all was well.

*

Back to the world of teenagers, I remember the nineteen year old I had the pleasure of meeting in Bristol. My wonderful daughter was at university there and I had popped down for the day to enjoy some mother daughter bonding time on her own turf. We were buying some unnecessary snacks at the cinema before taking our seats for the movie experience. I say unnecessary but what the heck, we all know how it is, the big screen outing is simply not the same without the additional high calorific intake is it?

The young man serving us just happened to be in the right place at the right time because I was happy and in a talkative mood, so told him that I had travelled down from London to enjoy the day with my daughter. I did not actually expect him to be the slighted bit interested, I just felt like saying it. As we made our choices my daughter persuaded me to change my mind over the selection of confectionary, so I said to the lad,

"Okay, I'll have what my daughter suggests, she is always right." This made him perk up. He looked at me and said,

"My mum never says that, I wish my mother would say that about me."

"Well, I say it because it's true, both of my children are always right. Are you always right?"

"I must be sometimes but no one ever notices."

Carole Chandler

"Of course you're right sometimes, you're probably right lots of times, I'm sure you are." He looked down and said to my utter amazement,

"I wish you were my mother." Well, how was I supposed to ignore him, poor love. I have no doubt that his mother is a wonderful person but that was hardly the issue so I said,

"Of course I can be your mother, what's your name?" Followed by, "I hereby adopt you, welcome to the family." My daughter was so funny, she took no notice of us whatsoever, she just let us continue our unusual chat like it was an everyday occurrence to hear someone her own age ask me to be his mother.

Just for the record, the film was not up to much, way too weird for my liking (and that is quite something coming from me) but it was great to spend time with my son's older sister.

So, babies, small children and teenagers are often a great source of amusement and frequently contribute towards a fun interaction. It has been enjoyable remembering a few episodes but now I feel inclined to return to the world of adult encounters.

*

But, but, but before I do that I was reminded today of how unusual my experiences are and how far I have come. A lovely young lady who I see occasionally told me that she was having a stressful day and had experienced a couple of 'run ins' with prickly characters in the same day, to use her words she felt like "a magnet for dodgy people." She also told me about a less than pleasant interaction with a mother and child at a bus stop during the weekend, so she was a bit fed up. She is a lovely girl and really one of the sweetest, kindest people I have ever met. She is always friendly and readily displays a loving, caring attitude towards people, so it was a real shame to hear her say that about herself.

I have frequently heard the question, 'why do bad things happen to good people?' and I have heard the answer too. It is hard to hear that we are responsible for things which happen to us, even the unwanted things but until we learn this we are powerless.

The things that were happening to her were just the kind of things which used to happen to me and they happened often. I can honestly say that they never happen now. She asked me how I managed to make it different and I started to share. She interrupted me, her thoughts were based on more than one false assumption and she was not ready to hear my response and that is okay. She is perfect as she is, she really does not need me and will make sense of the laws of the universe when she is ready.

I listened and she spoke, I listened some more. She had heard some things about vibration but when I attempted to say that everything is vibration she said,

"Carole, have you ever thought, do you ever think that you might be wrong?" I paused then said,

"I know that people might think differently." She was not satisfied with that so repeated,

"Yes but do you ever think that you might be wrong?" From my heart the only truthful answer I could give would be, no. As it happened I did not need to respond because at that moment someone called her away and she disappeared.

I had been challenged. My belief had been challenged, of course I thought about it. I thought about it for long enough to remind myself that there is nothing, absolutely nothing that disproves Universal Law. It matters not whether I think I am right or not, Universal Law just is. She had gone, so I did not even have the opportunity to quote Donald Shimoda and say, *"Some things are true whether we believe them or not."* By the way, Don can be found teaching in 'Illusions' author Richard Bach, a fantastic book and I highly recommend it.

I said it before and I say it again she really is a lovely lady, quite adorable every time I see her. She is now where I was years ago starting to ask questions. Why do people say horrible things when I am a nice person? Why are people unkind to me when I did not do anything wrong? Why are people unpleasant to me when I am just trying to help? I asked the question when the old lady said horrible things to me on the pavement in Guildford. I asked the question when the old man was nasty to me at Mortlake railway station. I asked the question when the van driver scared me with his temper in Wimbledon. I could go on, there were so many.

I had developed a portfolio of being at the receiving end of random acts of unpleasantness, which led me to believe that this was just how people were. Well yes, some are and some are not. One of my inspirations for writing these books is to share that strangers can be pleasant. I am not just lucky as people try to tell me. There is nothing special about me, well that is not strictly true because I am rather special, we are all special, we are all wonderful, we can all have the experiences that seem specific to me. I had to work at creating the change I wanted to be and as I have often said it is simple but not easy. It takes focus. For me it has been worth it. Each individual can decide whether it is worth the effort for them.

*

That is quite enough of the heavy stuff, now feels like a good time to return to the light hearted world, my world of meeting fun people. How about another day when I enjoyed some me time at the Royal Festival Hall. I had been there often on a Sunday morning and had a couple of favourite places to sit. On this particular day, I had spent the morning at home painting when at lunchtime, I felt the sudden impulse to take myself to the South Bank. My two o'clock arrival was new territory for me and was surprised to walk in and find the place heaving. I walked around looking for tables in my usual spots but they were all taken. I explored and discovered the fifth floor with the terrace and its fabulous view. I was delighted to find this lovely new area where I had not previously ventured.

Inside, I found the last available table, enjoyed my delicious soup, washed it down with my equally delicious peppermint tea and felt uber content in my own space, writing pages and pages of mood improving thoughts and feeling pretty good.

About forty minutes into my reverie I heard a voice,

"Excuse me." I looked up to see the handsome face of a gorgeous, radiant man, with bright brown eyes, smiling a heart-warming smile. Casually dressed, his clothes looked great on him and he seemed the perfect picture of health and happiness. I had probably already started to drool a little when he said,

"You probably don't remember me but you helped me at tango once." Well, if that was the case it must have been a while ago because for one reason and another I had not danced tango for ages. He confirmed, "Yes, it was four years ago, I remember it well, I remember where it was and I remember you because you were very kind to me when I was just a beginner." Oh my goodness, it was a huge compliment for me to listen to him talk about our previous meeting and what a difference it made to his early tango learning. I felt honoured. As any tango leader will tell you the early days can be challenging and I was delighted that he had found encouragement and support from my words and behaviour all those years ago. He flattered me by saying that his experience with me was the reason he kept going and now enjoys his passion for this intoxicating dance discipline.

The gorgeous Tango Man apologised for interrupting me and was about to leave but there was no way I wanted him to go anywhere. I invited him to join me, so he sat at my table and we talked about dancing and music and venues and dancing and more dancing. Something I found particularly joyful about him was the way he described his thoughts about the movements and music of Argentine tango. He referenced energy and the elements, wind, rain, rivers and oceans and I was really impressed. I know I talk like that but I do not meet many other people who do. He spoke so deliciously about our mutual interest and I adored hearing his passionate thoughts about improving his leading and understanding the importance of a relaxed follower, it was an absolute pleasure to chat to him. I also adored the way he listened to me so attentively, he seemed to overflow with genuine interest in my thoughts and opinions. I fell in love, well who wouldn't?

As with all good things, our conversation came to an end. Off he went leaving me with a warm fuzzy feeling which lasted for... ages.

So, a few things crossed my mind after that interaction. Firstly, I have no idea how he even recognised me out of context, where I was sitting, writing and concentrating with my head down. Secondly, I do not remember dancing with this gorgeous, lovely man four years ago but he remembers dancing with me. This is just another demonstration that we never know how we affect another. Thirdly, it was a positive experience and one I would never have known about, if we had not met again 'coincidentally' at the South Bank on that Sunday. Lastly, this meeting inspired me to return to tango, which inspired me to go on my Argentine tango holiday in Dublin, which inspired me to write my first book, which has inspired me to follow up with this one.

It begs the question, is anything really a question of chance?

*

I guess I should face it, this way of feeling good so much of the time as I do now, has the side effect of convincing me that I am falling in love with strangers quite often. Yes the Tango Man was special but I have fallen madly and deeply on other recent occasions too. I am reminded of the time I browsed in a pretty little shop in Covent Garden when I glanced around and was instantly smitten. He was looking and me and I was overjoyed to see that he continued to look at me as I gazed at him. Ooh, his beautiful eyes really had my attention and he stared like he did not care what anyone else thought. He stood beside a beautifully dressed young lady who was facing the other way, I could see they were together but I had no idea if they were attached. What would be her reaction if she saw him staring at me so intently?

He took a step towards me and I am not quite sure but I think that my heart missed a beat, I thought, "Oh my goodness he is coming over". My knees felt a little wobbly but I stayed still and he stepped closer, the girl turned around and wondered what he was looking at, she saw me and smiled. Phew, she did not mind then, so perhaps it would be okay for me to talk to him. We walked slowly towards each other and ooh, his big brown eyes were even more enchanting at close distance. Who was to speak first? I did not mind, the silent eye gazing was glorious enough for me and had already transported me to scenes from the famous Trevor Howard and Celia Johnson movie with bars of Rachmaninov somewhere in the distance.

He stared at me. I gazed at him. Time stood still. People moved around us but neither of us cared. I could have stayed there all day but something guided me to break the silence with,

"Wow, you're gorgeous." The lady who was with him thanked me and introduced us. Oh I was in heaven, he tilted his head, offered me his paw, I bent down and accepted.

It turned out that they were attached, by a beautiful gold lead which matched his gold collar decorated with diamante bones around it. She talked to me happily for a while in the shop and even proudly showed me some little tricks she had trained him to do. He was obedient and obviously intelligent, a proper little crowd pleaser and at that moment I was the crowd. It was an honour to meet them both. Did I fall hopelessly in love with this delightful cute little dog? Oh yes.

*

Moving far far away from the arena of infatuation, there was the time I stayed in a hotel for a few days and met a lovely chap who worked there. One day at breakfast we started chatting, easily and effortlessly it seemed. Within a surprisingly short space of time he was talking about energy, angels, attraction, guidance, value, worthiness, divinity, learning, teaching, knowing, allowing, connection and so many examples of awareness, that I became quite excited. He was speaking my language and it seemed to be such a chance encounter.

We talked for ages, he told me about his friendships, relationships, work, hopes and dreams. I was excited for him, for his bright future. Thankfully his colleagues did not seem to mind that we were amusing ourselves with lively conversation in the middle of the dining room. Our chat ended with a hug, a lovely hug, a warm body hug, a melting hug, he thanked me and I thanked him. He was truly delightful and it was an honour to meet him.

*

Next, let me take you to a supermarket in Wandsworth. So there I was wandering around, taking my time, minding my own business carrying my basket with a couple of items in it, standing by the veg counter, when a gentleman stopped beside me,

"Excuse me, may I ask you a question?" Well, lucky me, there I was yet again looking at the gorgeous face of a handsome man, with huge brown eyes, an engaging smile, tall, casually dressed, with his hat at a jaunty angle to complement his appearance. No, of course I had no objection to him asking me a question, he could ask anything he liked. However, whether I chose to answer or not remained to be seen. I kept all of that to myself and smiled.

"Do you know if they charge extra here to pay by credit card?" Really? Was that his question? What an odd question.

"No not at all, there is no charge. I don't know of any large supermarket chain which does that."

"Okay, thanks, I was just wondering." Oh really, is that what he was wondering? I returned my attention to the broccoli and noticed that he did not move away. I looked back, to find he was still watching me, still smiling his sweet smile. I could have wondered myself what he was wondering but feeling bold, I said,

"You didn't really need information about credit cards did you? You just wanted to talk to me." Ooh Carole, you saucy girl, how presumptuous of you to be so direct. Well it seemed only fair to just cut to the chase.

"Er, yes, I saw you walk past and I thought you looked lovely and I wanted to speak to you." I thanked him for the compliment and thought how nice it is to be noticed in a positive light. He looked in my basket and asked if I was buying food for anything in particular. I laughed and told him that my son had been complaining about the food I give him (which was true), so I was buying ingredients for him to make his own meal from his new Levi Roots cookery book, as he had been inspired by Levi's style and television programme. He sighed and said whimsically,

"Aah, a Roots man, a lion in a concrete jungle." Ooh, I liked that, I promised to tell my boy that I had met him and share his phrase. He said it with a deliciously strong Caribbean accent, which really needs to be heard to be appreciated and sadly I am unable to do it justice on these pages. He introduced himself, asked my name, took my hand, shook it and held it with both of his hands for longer than was absolutely necessary, or customary considering the brevity of our acquaintance.

We chatted about this and that, he maintained his lovely smile, I liked the way he looked into my eyes, it was lovely to meet him and I was flattered by his attention. When I felt it was time to move on, I made my excuses and left.

*

It seems that people frequently find excuses to talk to me in supermarkets. Once I waited by the checkout in one of my local stores and a woman shuffled up to me with her basket half filled with a variety of cola bottles and cans. We smiled at each other and without me asking, she launched into a detailed explanation of why she was armed with a selection of fizzy drinks. Apparently, her daughter had requested a particular version of a specified brand but as she could not find it, this woman had decided to buy a few others, to see if she might be successful in changing her daughter's allegiance. I wished her luck. She was doing more than I would. If one of my children had requested something so specific, I would not consider buying an alternative. I would sooner return with nothing and let them sort it out for themselves.

Experience and awareness of everyone's ability to choose has taught me a lot. She was in danger of finding herself in a situation of perceived ungratefulness. Just like the time I was on one of my residential meditation weekends, this time in sunny Wiltshire. None of us knew each other, we were just individuals on a course to try and make sense of the world and improve our lives.

A few of us sat under a canopy in the garden after lunch, when one of the chaps offered to pop to the kitchen and make hot drinks. He asked for requests and a beautiful young lady, who he had already been paying a fair amount of attention to, asked for a lemon and ginger herbal tea. He returned with a tray and gave her a cup saying that he could not find what she had requested so he made her a peppermint tea with a slice of lemon. He looked jolly pleased with himself and everything would have been fine, if she liked peppermint tea but she did not. He called her ungrateful. She was clearly upset. I felt her pain.

I gently pointed out that he asked her what she wanted, she gave her choice, he brought something that she did not ask for, that does not make her ungrateful. It was an unfortunate situation but I have been on both sides of that fence. It felt like a good idea at the time to speak for her, so I did. She thanked me. Later he stopped me in the house and he thanked me for giving him a new perspective. All was well.

*

So back to the world of supermarkets, a lady in front of me at a checkout in Tooting commented on my basket of fruit and vegetables. She compared them with her cakes and biscuits on the conveyer belt. She felt guilty but I assured her that there was really no need. I do eat cakes and biscuits too and I have a particular weakness for custard creams and almond croissants. She picked up her box of muffins and waved them in front of my face clearly wanting me to take a closer look, telling me that they were her husband's favourite and as it was his birthday she was treating him. How sweet of her to share all that with me.

Another time I found myself in a long queue in a small supermarket in Victoria when a woman and small child joined the line behind me. They were tourists to our wonderful capital having flown in from the USA that very morning. They were both quite delightful and clearly excited. Then the mother looked in her basket, realised she had forgotten something, announced that she was leaving her child with me and disappeared out of sight. Er, okay. Not much to say about that really.

*

My supermarket experiences seem to be plentiful and I have a lot of fun with cashiers who often are keen to engage in a little more than "do you have a nectar card?" In a new little one near my home this very question prompted some fun dialogue. I keep my nectar card on my key ring, which is handy because I always have my keys, or so I thought. The chap processed the items, requested the card and totally out of character, my keys were nowhere to be found. I was not sure what to think as I am not a, 'where are my keys', 'where is my card' kind of person. I always know where my things are, yet for some reason they were evading me.

"Well, I don't seem to have my card because I don't seem to have my keys, so more interestingly, I'm not sure how I'm going to get in if my son's gone out."

"Oh, so you might be stranded then?"

"I think that's a distinct possibility, so if you see me wandering the streets when you finish work ..." He appeared to be heartily amused by the prospect and his parting words were,

"Hope you find a bed for the night!" What joker.

*

Then there was the chatty lady behind a till in a supermarket in Victoria. It is often a handy place for me to shop on my way home from central London because the bus which takes me home, leaves from directly across the road. All I have to do is risk my life dodging buses, vans and taxis to cross the road and I am fine.

Anyway, I bought a few bits and asked for fifty quid cash back. The cashier dispensed advice,

"Don't spend it all at once", to which I said,

"Oh don't worry it's already spent darling. I have a son who spends it for me."

She asked how old he was then wittily proceeded to tell me her opinion about sons and how they never grow up and how they are always little boys and how they love to spend money and how they love their mothers. I did not say much in response but then again I did not need to because she seemed happy sharing her thoughts. Her colleague at the adjacent checkout joined in, he agreed with her and was happy to admit to never growing up. We had a proper Peter Pan in the house.

*

Then there was the young cashier in our local store in Earlsfield long before they extended it to be the big little supermarket that it is now. He was a young lad probably early twenties with impeccable manners and a neatly cropped afro which looked recently trimmed, emphasising his handsome face and clear smooth skin.

When he handed over my change, I was immediately distracted by his gorgeous hand with long elegant fingers. It would have been difficult not to notice and me being me, I felt compelled to say something. I asked for a closer look as I complimented him. He kindly let me have both to view then saying he felt embarrassed hid both hands behind his back. Well that was fine, he did not have to show me his hands if he did not want to but I suggested that it seemed a pity not to be proud of such beautiful hands and fingers.

"Are you an artist or a musician? With fingers like yours, I suspect you are." He denied it. I felt inspired to persist, "Really! I'm surprised. You don't play an instrument?" Negative. "You don't paint or draw either?"

"Well, I used to draw a lot when I was younger but I stopped."

"There you go, I thought so. I'll bet you were good at it too, right?" He shrugged and given his age, I took that as a yes. "Well it might be an idea to take it up again, you probably have a gift and it seems a shame to waste those artistic hands." He stopped hiding them, looked at them and smiled to himself. It was a pleasure for me to see him looking so pleased.

Carole Chandler

"You sound like my sister, she's always saying that to me."

"Well, your sister sounds like a clever lady, so you can tell her that you met me and I agreed with her." Who knows, perhaps he is travelling the world exhibiting his artistic creations as a result of our short interaction.

*

Then there was the lovely lady in a supermarket in Kingston. I commented on her pretty, pink, sparkly, heart shaped watch and as it was March, I wondered if it were a Valentine's gift from an adoring partner. She laughingly told me that she bought it for herself and explained her amusement because her husband would never consider buying her anything for Valentine or birthday or anniversaries or any other kind of celebration for that matter. Interesting.

She told me that he does not believe in buying gifts for her and she has learned not to expect any. Interesting. How did she feel about that? She said that it was not really the way she wanted things to be but seeing as they had been married a long time, she supposed it was unreasonable to expect anything more. Interesting.

Then as if talking about something else completely, she told me excitedly that it was soon to be their thirtieth wedding anniversary. While I was happy that she saw it as cause for celebration, I did not share her excitement. It just brought back memories of the times I have celebrated longevity just for the sake of it.

I used to find it interesting that people are willing to tolerate all kinds of relationships. Now I know better. Now I know that it is the relationship with myself which is the only one that matters then all the others click effortlessly into place.

*

Then there was the lovely young lady in a little supermarket in Wimbledon Broadway, I looked at her name badge and asked her if that was actually her name. Wow, yes her name really was Peace. How wonderful is that? To be named Peace, to have parents who even thought of a name like that, to go through life with the name Peace. She looked peaceful which was nice. She said she liked her name and I was glad for her.

Then there was the lovely lady in the large supermarket in Tooting Broadway, I looked at her name badge and asked what her Asian name meant, she said that he means Love. How wonderful is that? To have a name that means love. To have parents who even thought of giving her a name that means love, to go through life with a name that means love. She looked lovely which was nice. She said she liked her name and I was glad for her.

*

Then there was the checkout lady in the Tooting store who commented on my shopping bags. I understood her delight, they are quite beautiful and that is why I use them. I have two red ones with white polka dots and two blue ones with strawberries on them. I am not one for the colour orange about my person. I do not own any orange items of clothing or accessories, so I do not choose to carry orange plastic bags. People think I am being environmentally friendly but I take my own bags simply because they coordinate better with me.

Comments are frequently made about my bags so I told her what I tell everyone,

"If I have to go shopping, I may as well make it fun and these bags are much more fun than the plastic ones." They always agree.

Then there was the happy chappy behind the till in another store when I was buying a few bits with my daughter for company. As all cashiers do these days he asked if I needed a bag. I proudly whisked out one of my red and white spotty ones and announced,

"I have brought my own bag, my pretty bag." He laughed and said,

"A pretty bag for a pretty lady." Ooh er, what a charmer, I wonder if he says that to all the girls? He was in a good mood and I was in a good mood so I said,

"Oh, how sweet of you, that's a lovely thing to say." He told me he said it because it was true but there was no need for clarification because I was not about to argue.

He must have meant it because when I gave him my loyalty card he said

"I'm giving you points for using your own bag and double points because you're a beautiful lady." Oh bless him. There was no need for any of that but it was lovely of him to think of it. When he gave me my receipt he went to the trouble of showing me that the double points had been added purely because he liked me. What a sweetie.

*

Then there was my visit to the supermarket within the shopping centre in Wandsworth. I still want to call it the Arndale because that is what it was called for ages but now it is the Southside, so I guess I can cope with the name change. The lovely cheerful Oriental gentleman who processed my shopping seemed to be quite excited when he saw my bag. Their plastic bags may not be orange but I do not wear a lot of green either, so chose to stay with my favoured coordination. He liked the colour red and in particular the white spots. He said,

"I like the spots on your bag", I like them too and had always considered them to be just polka dots until he said, "In my country that pattern means prosperity." Wow, that was good to hear and I thanked him for sharing this nugget of information with me. With the help of everything I had been learning, I had worked on improving my beliefs around the subject of abundance, so his words were just another clue that I was doing something right.

*

Then there was the supermarket employee who asked me if I wanted to use the self-service checkout. Well just for the record, the answer to that question will always be no. I do not care how long the queue is for a real person at a till. I do not care how many self-service checkout points are available. I do not care how few items I have. I am not interested in using the self-service option. They have proven to be an unnecessarily stressful waste of my time and energy. What is the point when a member of staff invariably has to bail you out anyway as a result of some problem or other? I am led to believe that important busy people use them for speed but I am never in that much of a hurry. When she asked me I smiled and said,

"I'll come over if you are happy to do it."

"Don't you like using them?"

"Let's just say I prefer not to."

"That's okay, I'll put them through for you."

"You'll stay and do all of it and wait until I've paid and got my change, you won't run off if someone else has a problem?" Well it would have made no difference to me if she had decided to retract her offer, I was quite happy to stay where I was. Yes, I was in a queue but I would have been served eventually and time is an illusion anyway. Ooh, I have just realised that this is the first time I have mentioned the illusion that is time in this book, I made several references to it in my book about meeting strangers in Ireland.

Carole Chandler

Allow me to indulge myself for a moment while I remember an occasion when I announced, that 'time is an illusion' during a conversation at a meal table during one of my jive dance holidays. Sitting beside me was a lady I had not met before and when she heard me make that statement, she became quite excited. Her husband was sitting opposite and in conversation with another gentleman. She interrupted him, demanding that he stop talking and listen to what I had to say. She insisted I repeat it, she really wanted him to hear. I thought it was quite amusing because she could have just as easily said the words herself but no, she was determined that he should hear it from me. With the fuss that she was making, everyone else at the table stopped talking too and all eyes were on me. I said it again and she said to her man,

"There did you hear that, did you, I hope you heard that, I told you." Another lady shouted from the other end of the table,

"Age is an illusion too." Of course I agreed with her and said,

"Yes you're right because age is just another definition of time so it's the same."

The comments did not last long because we were soon talking about other matters. I suppose there was not the time to spend more time talking about time.

Anyway, back to the lady at the supermarket self-service checkout. While I had finished issuing my list of demands, the lovely lady was laughing and had taken my basket over to the vacant self-checkout zone. She behaved like she actually wanted to do it for me. I could have probably found myself a chair and could have probably had a little sit down and she probably would not have objected, well probably. She was delightful and happy in her work and I felt the inspiration to say,

"Thank you for helping me, you're an angel." What I did not expect her to say was,

"That's my daughter's name." What did she mean?

"I have a little girl and her name is Angel." Well, she had to be kidding me. I nearly cried. I had already been bowled over by the name Peace and here it was being trumped by the name Angel. I asked questions, lots of questions. This lovely, lovely lady did not seem to mind at all. Yes her daughter's name was Angel. Yes, she is actually called Angel. No, it is not a pet name. Yes, that is the name she has had from birth. Yes, it is an unusual name. Yes, it was her idea. Yes, she is the perfect description of her name. Yes, she is a fortunate little girl to be going through life with such a beautiful name. Yes, the name does encourage people to treat her in a certain way.

Seriously folks, how can anyone say that a name does not matter? How can it not? Do not get me started on some of the obscurities which I came across during my neonatal nursing days. Moving on.

*

I have had numerous encounters of an angelic persuasion which I may feel guided to share in a later publication. We shall see. For now I shall maintain my focus in this dimension and remind myself about the young man who came into our shop once when I sat at my little hand massage table.

If I had seen him years ago, I would have been quite likely to maintain my distance. His demeanour was not displaying a "hey let's chat" kind of attitude. That may be the reason why the people I was talking to, walked away when he approached. Not me, I do not worry about the image that people think they are presenting. I look beneath it, sometimes a long way beneath it. That is sometimes where the real person is, deep down. We often live inside a barrier, protection whatever we choose to call it. I did it for most of my life and love the fact that I do not need to protect myself any more. Interestingly a client said this week,

"The way you look at me, it's as though you are looking into my soul." I like to think that on some level, she knew that to be the truth and this may be why she said she felt better even before her treatment began. People describe me using the words peace and tranquillity and I could not ask for more than that. I have learned that deep down everyone wants to love and be loved, no matter how unapproachable they may appear to be.

As this young chap walked past me, his bare right arm caught my attention. It was decorated with a tattoo of a wing, just a wing, a long wing. Interesting. I boldly said,

"Hey, look at you with your wing tattoo." He paused and without looking at his face I stood up to walk around him saying, "Do you have one on the other arm too?"

"Yes there is, otherwise I'd fly around in circles all the time." Ha ha, so there was nothing to be concerned about after all, Mr Wingman had a sense of humour that he was happy to display.

"Good point, I guess you've used that line few times." He shrugged and given his age I took that as a yes. I was having fun, so I continued, "You must be an angel then." He grunted and replied,

"I don't know about that." I was still having fun so I continued, "Of course you are and you've got the wings to prove it. So whose angel are you then?" By then he was actually facing me and not head down in an I-dare-you-to-look-at-me attitude like when he came in.

"I would never presume that I am someone's angel."

"Well, perhaps you should." I do not use the word 'should' often for obvious reasons but it felt appropriate at the time. They were my final words and I think, maybe, perhaps, I just think that I might have spotted a teeny weeny hint of a smile before he walked away.

*

Another tattoo inspired interaction occurred in a Richmond petrol station. As I walked in, it was impossible not to notice a man at the front by the counter. He was noticeable because of the volume which he had selected for communication. Why was he shouting? Simple really, he was talking to his friend who was still in their car, so of course he had to ramp up the decibels in an attempt to make himself heard from the shop, through the window, across the forecourt, through the car window to his mate within the vehicle. There is hardly any point mentioning that the car window was closed because the pal would have struggled to hear either way.

So there was this young man at the front of the shop and causing a bit of a stir as far as I could see. The short walk I made from the entrance up to the counter gave me an opportunity to not only hear him shouting but also witness some choice language. Perhaps this was his normal vocabulary when conversing with peers but it is not mine. Also, bearing in mind we were in Richmond, I suspect some people may have had an opinion or two. Anyway, he was not talking to me, so I let it be.

I stood behind him and waited, there was someone being served before him, so his shouting and peppered language continued. I guess it may be considered swearing for some but normal for others, they are just words after all. It was bordering on the ridiculous really because of course his buddy had no hope of hearing him. Never mind, he laughed raucously and gave the definite impression that he was having fun and probably did not care what anyone thought.

I suspect that he was not the kind of chap who is accustomed to being challenged. Oh no, definitely not. Young, tall, cropped spikey brown hair, a highly developed upper body, clad in a plain white vest. Yes a vest, not a t-shirt, not a sleeveless sports top but a vest. It brings to mind the wonderful line delivered by the comic genius David Hyde Pierce as his character Niles in the unparalleled American situation comedy, 'Frasier'. He says, "Daphne deserves someone for whom a vest is an undergarment." Oh how I love that show and it was right up there at the top of my list equal to my adoration of 'Black Adder' series two and three. Well that was until I discovered 'The Big Bang Theory'. Magic. I discovered all these shows long after other people so hooray for repeats on cable television.

Anyway, back to the loud, tall, hench, vest wearing dude, who animatedly accompanied his communication attempts with a collection of arm gesticulations, waving vigorously making signs and laughing. The active arm waving drew my attention to his body illustrations. His muscular arm was decorated and I was distracted. My eyes were on his arm and my head was following his movements, when he spotted me. He stopped shouting. He lowered his arm. He looked at me. I looked up at him and smiled. Well, who was to know which way it could have gone? He was twice my size with a highly dubious temperament and perhaps I was taking a chance by even risking eye contact with this character. Never mind, I was already becoming familiar with how events and circumstances turn out for me, when I allow myself to be me and allow love to flow from within. I was unconcerned and just felt inspired to do what felt right at the time. I had no idea what he was going to say. He had clearly seen me looking at him and we have all heard stories about how that can affect a situation. Well would you believe it, as I smiled he stepped back and said,

"After you." Well that was unexpected. He gestured politely, inviting me to be served before him. The wild lion had instantly transformed to a cute kitten. I do not know what came over me but instead of just accepting the invitation and take the opportunity to be on my way, I returned my attention to his arm and said,

"Thanks but I'm distracted by your tattoos." He seemed surprised and I continued,

"Stand still a moment", while I tilted my head and scanned round him. He just stood there quietly and let me amuse myself. When I had entertained myself for long enough, I paused to look up at his somewhat bemused, yet slightly amused face and said, "They're actually very good." That was it, my work was done. He paid for his petrol and left without another peep from him. Admittedly that was not my goal if indeed I had one at all. However it was interesting to observe his change in demeanour and behaviour in that short period of time. By the way, I was just kidding when I said I do not know what came over me, I know exactly what came over me, I saw beauty and felt like acknowledging it.

*

I called the vest wearer a kitten but perhaps I should have said puppy which would have led seamlessly to my canine interactions. They too have been plentiful and interesting.

From a young age I had a fear of dogs, any dog, all dogs, large or small. I had it drummed into me that they are dangerous, unpredictable, worthy of my apprehension and not to be trusted. Repeated news reports about dogs and their unwanted activities involving members of the public, also went a long way towards maintaining my mistrust and of course, being bitten on the ankle by a Jack Russell when I was eight years old, just succeeded in feeding my concerns.

I had moved mountains when it came to relationships, all relationships, family, friends, brief acquaintances and strangers. I gradually came to understand that the positive changes extended towards animals too. I shall resist the temptation to retell the glorious swan incident from my previous book, no matter how tempted I am to include it here.

A few years ago I was on a residential meditation weekend in the countryside of Cheltenham. We were enjoying glorious weather and I was basking in the effects of the meditation techniques led by our particularly gifted teacher. We were a group of about twenty people, gathered with our wide ranging personalities and interests. At the time I could not understand how members of the group were going through some of the intensely challenging lives which they were living. Now I understand that we all had something to learn, we all had something to teach and we all had something to contribute.

It was lunchtime and we had finished eating and most of us were enjoying a chat sitting together as one collection around a long table, with one seat at each end and about ten seats down each side. The French doors were open with a view out to the terrace and gardens, when someone noticed a dog walk in. The little dog wandered in and the question of who he belonged to went around the room. Seemingly, he did not belong to any of us, so not much happened at the time. He slowly walked along the full length of the table on the opposite side to me, walked around the person on the single seat at the end, proceeded down my side, reached my seat and stopped. The dog looked up at me. I looked down at him not thinking much about it, when he put his paw on my thigh. He was just the cutest little creature ever with gorgeous, huge, brown eyes. With his two paws now on my leg I said,

"Hallo there, have I been chosen?" Some people laughed saying that he must have been looking for me, which I enjoyed hearing.

I invited him on to my lap where he sat and allowed me to stroke him until we left. When the group dispersed I carried him around for a while until a lady claimed him. She did not mind him being with me but she objected to me holding him. She apparently did not want him to get used to being picked up and certainly did not allow him to sit on laps. She felt strongly about it and told me so. Interesting. I just saw holding him as one of the many displays of affection, a way of giving and receiving love.

We took him for a walk and she talked at length about the hurt she was experiencing in her family and partner relationships. It appeared that the theme of withholding affection continued and was not limited to her relationship with her pet. I guess she was not alone because we all had work to do.

*

I am reminded of a non-dog but baby related incident, which I feel inclined to include here because it concerns the withholding of affection. It happened when I worked as a neonatal nurse in our transitional care unit, which was a section for babies well enough to stay with the mother but not well enough to go home. Mostly in single rooms it proved to be surprisingly fulfilling work for me, as I had the advantage of working closely with new families, bringing me much joy.

One day I walked into a room and also into a highly charged, tense atmosphere indeed. The mother was sitting on the bed, crying. The baby was in his cot, crying. The father was sitting on the other side of the room with his arms folded, scowling. Oh dear.

Clearly something was adrift and I was there to help if possible. It transpired that their two day old baby had started to cry, mother wanted to pick him up because he was crying and her husband had told her not to pick him up because he was crying. Why not? Apparently his mother had taught him that it is wrong to pick up a baby when he cries. Why not? Apparently, it will spoil him. What does that even mean?

My purpose, my intention, my goal is never to question whether his mother is right, or whether he is right, or whether the unhappy lady on the bed is right, or whether the unhappy baby in the cot is right. So, when they asked me what I thought I said that I appreciate that there are lots of opinions about the rights and wrongs of picking up a crying baby. I looked at the mother and simply expressed a perspective,

"Your baby is two days old, he is upset, now you are upset. Decide how you feel and you decide if it feels better to pick him up or not." I looked at the father and expressed a perspective,

"Your mother had her reasons based on her experiences. This is your baby and your wife, you can decide what feels right for all of you here and now." The lady picked up her baby, she comforted him, her husband unfolded his arms, the cloud lifted, the tension dissipated. All was well.

I could have said lots about varying forms of communication, about babies, children, adults and dogs for that matter. I could have said lots about ways of asking for attention and having our needs ignored. Yes, I do have opinions about it, we all do. I am now quick to offer affection, I am quick to offer attention, I understand the value. Now as a result I receive attention and affection too. I am in a much better position now with my understanding of who I am.

I am not quite sure why but at this point I feel the urge to say a few words about my dancing experiences perhaps by way of highlighting some examples of receiving attention. Off the dance floor I was miserable, unloved, unseen and unheard. On the dance floor I was noticed, I attracted a lot of attention. It was hard to make sense of it but it was fun all the same. I was unavailable and men flirted mercilessly with me. Some of them had no shame and I trod a fine line between being flattered and being insulted. Either way it was attention and that was infinitely better than being ignored.

Social dancing is all about meeting and communicating with strangers. I have enjoyed it for years and could write volumes about my experiences however revisiting some of my earlier encounters would be in danger of bringing me out of my happy positive place. I do know that I learned a lot about myself, the environment taught me how it was possible to feel good and I particularly learned how to set and maintain boundaries. Also it was a fantastic arena for me to learn the power of knowing what I want and deciding why I want it.

When my circumstances changed, I became available and I went back to some of the lovely guys who had appeared to show so much interest. What was the result? Well, just imagine Wile E Coyote from the Warner Bros Looney Toons cartoons. He is known for disappearing in a cloud of dust and they did pretty much the same, although in my case the dust was more imaginary as our dance venues do not much resemble the Arizona desert. Anyway, these guys (bless them) disappeared in a cloud of something, I have seldom seen people run so fast and with them went some of my lovely dances too. One of the cutest guys on the circuit, who had often paid me a certain level of non-dance related attention, made me laugh a couple of years ago. We had not seen each other for a while, so it was great to bump into him again at one of our popular Saturday night venues. It was no surprise when he asked what I had been up to and when I mentioned my change of status he said,

"So Carole, now that you are available, I guess that means you're on the look-out for casual sex." Well that was news to me. Clearly I had not paid due attention to my copy of the government information leaflet, 'Ten Things You Should Know Now That You Are Available', or perhaps I had not received the updated version. Never mind, I think I am managing quite well without it. Years ago his implication may have made some sense to me but not now, not now that I have learned the value of adoring myself and have tasted the sweet deliciousness of a life that feels good. Given his opening line, I had my suspicions that our conversation would not have far to go but I thought I would amuse myself for a moment and go with the flow. My response to him was,

"Not at all, in fact far from it."

"Really!" He looked and sounded genuinely surprised, "aren't you looking for people to get naked, hot and sweaty with?" Oh bless his dancing shoes, he was cute but not that cute. If his chiselled jaw line, fashionably cropped hair, slim physique and princely posture were not enough to persuade me, then his current unflattering turn of phrase was not going to do it for me. Of course I liked him but what he said did not ring my bell.

I am reminded of a lovely lady I met in London a couple of years ago, we became great friends and socialised about town having fun and laughing a lot in each other's company. She seemed to enjoy my stories of meeting people and it appears that she misunderstood my tales about attention from guys. She invited me to her family home on the other side of the world and offered to find me a handsome local. I thought nothing of it and simply said that I was not interested in a long distance relationship. The intention was made clear when she said, that she was not thinking of relationship but just a one night stand for fun and blah blah blah. She too seemed surprised when I told her that I was not looking for fast food but had my sights set on more of a Michelin star rated gourmet dining experience.

I have a high tolerance level and a broad mind. Life is a veritable smorgasbord of entertainment and experiences and we all get to make our own choices to suit our individual tastes. I have little interest in what people choose to do or why they choose to do it. I appreciate that casual sex has its place and serves people well, as a useful form of expression. However, until I can believe it to be positive experience for me, then I shall respectfully decline. The 'how about it' approach, is not what I am looking for. The 'click your fingers and I'll come running' approach, is not going to work either. If I change my mind then that will be okay too.

So back to my handsome dancer, I was happy for him to share his naked, hot and sweaty views but I had lost interest already so I said,

"No thanks, you'll have to marry me first." His response was instant, humorous and conclusive,

"Nah, that's too much foreplay." There was no need for him to do the coyote impression, I left, message understood.

I am delighted to say that my dancing experiences now are all superb. No longer do I encounter any of the sexually repressed nonsense of yesteryear. I am paid the most delightful compliments with alarming regularity, encountering gentlemanly and appropriate behaviour at all times, everyone is charming and polite without exception. It is always fun, fun, fun, no concerns, just fun. I continue to meet amazing people and who would have guessed that I would stumble across a spiritual salsa teacher? It would be no surprise at tango but I did not expect to find a salsa instructor who regularly says, "Practise, practise, practise until you find the truth!" I thought it was my imagination the first time I heard him but have been amused to hear him repeat it often in his wonderful classes.

Here is a delightful example of something lovely that a chap said to me on one of my many dance floors, a couple of months ago. I was at a friendly salsa venue and enjoying a fabulous moment of spinning and twirling, led by a gloriously, skilled, accomplished leader. I had met him a couple of times before but did not know his name or anything about him. We had never had a conversation except for the word free communication which takes place during the music. (Perhaps I may devote a whole book to talking to strangers in that arena.) As ever the end came all too soon, we thanked each other, he said lovely complimentary things about my following and I expressed my adoration of his leading proficiency. I ended by calling him a genius and was about to let him go, when he said,

Carole Chandler

"Even a genius needs a canvas on which to create," he paused then added, "and you are the perfect canvas." WOW! Perhaps I was lost for words and perhaps I lost my mind just a little bit. What a lovely thing for him to say and for me to hear. To be honest I think I fell in love (again). Come on, when a guy looks that good and dances that well and says those words, no one could blame me for falling in love, could they? People wonder why I dance. Need I say more?

I am blessed.

*

Well, after that protracted digression, I return to my canine encounters. A fairly early experience with a dog was during a long walk in the rain across a muddy path in Richmond Park. One of the most beautiful places probably in the world and I was fortunate enough to live less than a mile away for over twenty years. I never took the beauty for granted and enjoyed cycling or walking there every day. My children on the other hand were always a bit blasé about seeing resident deer in the park. Just like all the local children, seeing deer was an everyday occurrence for them so what was all the fuss about? They sometimes wondered why people were stopping to take pictures on a sunny Sunday afternoon. They were just deer after all. The last couple of years before we moved I walked there much more. I explored more. I rediscovered the park, while I rediscovered myself. Cycling had always been to keep fit, then I discovered that walking was more meditative. Walking on the grass, away from the tracks, amongst the trees and shrubs, greatly increased my opportunities to find my emotional balance, be grounded and to be connected.

It was a wet day and I walked with a long row of trees on my left and a large field on my right, with the road so far away that the cars were not even audible. A woman came into view way, way ahead of me. She was wearing a Barbour, well every other person wears a Barbour in that area. I even tried wearing one twenty odd years ago in an effort to fit in. It seems comical now. Beside her walked a little sand coloured dog. Yes, yes, I know that sand is red in Paignton and black in Tenerife but I am talking about regular coloured Hawaiian Islands and Isle of Wight kind of sand. As they came closer, her companion left her side and scampered towards me. He stopped by my feet and looked up with beautiful, big, brown eyes. I had stopped walking too and I had his attention until his lady caught up with us.

I commented on his friendliness and she said that she had never known him to walk up to a stranger like that before. I was flattered of course I was, he was truly delightful and clearly thought I was okay too. I bent down to stroke him and he raised his front paws to rest them on my knee. She told him to stop and get down and apologised for his muddy paws but I was totally unconcerned about a bit of dirt. I assured her that it would wash off and simply thought to myself that I was happy to make his acquaintance, in true Jane Austen fashion.

As I continued to make a fuss of him, it felt only natural to tell him that he was gorgeous and it was understandable that he enjoyed the attention and loved being stroked. I asked her what breed he was and she told me. I have no idea why I even asked because I cannot remember what she said and I know very little about one breed compared to another, except for Westies but I shall come to them later. When I told her that I did not know much about dogs, she expressed surprise and said that she would never have guessed, as I seemed so comfortable with her little chap.

It was all good. For me that meeting was another clue that I must have been doing something right.

*

Then there was the time I was just turning into Richmond Park's Sheen Gate when a woman wearing a long red rain coat, came out with a Westie. Well, I may not know many breeds but I do know a West Highland Terrier when I see one. It is distinctly possible that they may be the cutest ever. I have had dreams about owning one (or three), so when I spotted this woman I suddenly felt the urge to ask her what they are like to live with. What on earth was I thinking? Surely there are other ways to find out about life with a Westie. Surely you do not just walk up to a stranger and ask questions about her pet. Whether I was right or wrong really does not matter now because I did stop her and I did ask her and she did not seem to object at all. She was happy to tell me the pros and cons of having him share their family life.

*

Then there was the delightful couple I met while living in my luxury new development. I only met them because I always recognised their dog. He was the most stylish, yes I said stylish Westie I have ever seen, with the best name ever. Embarrassingly, I would see the dog but not recognise the owner, either the chap or the lady until I had met them several times. I also had a habit of greeting the little chap and making an almighty fuss of him and soaking up the attention I received from him too, before I would remember to greet his owner. Thankfully I have improved my manners and stopped doing that. They were just the loveliest people and both really friendly, yet I also kept on forgetting their names and sincerely hoped that they did not notice. This divine four legged creature always greeted me with joyful enthusiasm like he had known me forever. It warmed my heart whenever I had the pleasure of meeting him and the warm fuzzy feeling would stay with me for hours.

One day I boldly knocked on their door and asked if I could join them for a walk some time. I was so glad that the idea was well received, so with the date and time agreed, I skipped home excitedly and told my children that I was in love and going on a date. My daughter was not fooled for a moment and calmly asked if I had met my beloved canine friend again. My son on the other hand was horrified,

"You can't just invite yourself out for a walk with their dog." Perhaps he was right but I did not care and I was too excited to worry about it.

On the 'date' the three of us walked to a nearby park where the guy warned me to beware of two wolf hounds which had spotted us across the street. He had experienced problems with them before when they had been less than friendly with his pet. I scanned them and sensed no concern so felt content saying that I thought it would be fine and that they did not mean any harm. Yet, he was still uncomfortable and wanted to leave the area. We walked elsewhere for a bit then returned, entered the park from another gate walked for a short while, then saw the two hounds again. By the way, they were beautiful, elegant creatures, looking resplendent in their silver, grey and black coats with their pointed faces and knowing eyes. The two of them caught wind of us from the other side of the field and started to walk slowly, directly towards us. My canine companion seemed okay but my human companion tensed,

"Oh look, they're coming, there is going to be trouble, let's go." I was not having that. If I am to believe the laws of the universe and I do, if I am believe in my well-being and I do, if I am to believe that our meetings are all about energy and I do, then I believed that I could stay, we could stay and all would be well. I said,

"We're fine, they are not going to bother him, not today. They don't mean any harm."

I have no idea what happened, I have no idea why they changed their minds but when I stopped right where we were and looked at them, the dogs stopped too. They clearly had second thoughts because one turned around and walked in the opposite direction while the other turned left and ran off to the other side of the field.

We all learned a lot that day.

*

Then there was the time I enjoyed an early cycle ride in Wandsworth Common. I stopped to allow a woman with two dogs to cross my path but instead of walking on, she stopped to exchange pleasantries. It was 6.30am and she had already been walking her dogs for an hour. I thought I was a morning person so I was impressed with her even earlier start. We talked about the beauty of that part of the day and she seemed to be concerned for the people who miss it by getting up late. She is absolutely right, the mornings can be so incredible beautiful. I have been treated to the sight of an early morning rainbow and looked around to find no one to share it with. That never matters though because I know the joy is mine to savour as much as I choose. I have been rendered speechless by the exquisite colours of a morning sky particularly by the deep shade of pink which nature can create to accompany the familiar blue. It cannot be captured on camera, I have tried and I am convinced that if someone tried to recreate it on canvass, people would find the colour combination unreal.

One of her dogs ran off then ran back repeatedly, the other dog went nowhere. I had fun chatting with her as she explained that the little one was young and excitable while the quiet one was old and slow. I had paid little attention to the fact that she had a buggy with her but all was revealed when she volunteered to tell me that it was for the mature pet when he ran out of energy. The little frisky chap needed much more exercise so when the other could not keep up with the pace, she would put him in the seat. That way she could still enjoy the walk and not slow the little one down. How thoughtful is that? I also loved her telling me all this because I had never come across those dynamics before and found it interesting.

I have no idea how many people would hold such a conversation with a stranger at that time of the morning in an out of the way place like that. I took it as a real compliment.

*

Then there was the day I visited a new client at her home. She opened the door and before she greeted me, I was met by her little, thin legged, short haired, tan coloured dog which decided to bark, as well as either jump up at me or snap at my heels. The owner issued a few half-hearted, 'there there, stop it, don't do that, behave yourself' kind of instructions, but the dog continued. I entered, we tried to talk but it was not easy with her dog's persistent poor behaviour. It was intensely irritating and not to be tolerated.

I have learned to love dogs but I also know when enough is enough. With this animal being tiresome around my legs, I paused the conversation we were trying to have, looked down at her pest, I mean pet and said,

"I am not going to take any notice of you while you behave like this. Come back and see me when you are ready to be sensible." I sat down at the table with my client, while we conversed over cups of tea. The dog wandered about, not snapping, not barking, not jumping, just thinking. After a few minutes, our four legged companion returned to me, stood by my seat and looked up. I said,

"That's much better, I'm ready to take notice of you now." We continued our human conversation, while the dog put her paws on my leg, I stroked her back, I invited her on to my lap, where she curled up and went to sleep.

I have no idea who was more astonished. My client said that the dog's behaviour which I had been treated to upon arrival, was the way she had always been and attempts to change her had failed. She also said that she normally shuts her away in another room when strangers come. Interesting. Why had she not shut her in another room when I came? Who knows? Anyway, she thanked me for calming her dog down and I was quietly, inwardly grateful for the experience to learn more about myself. Life is good.

*

Then there was the time I enjoyed another lovely muddy walk in the rain on Wandsworth Common. Just for the record, I do a lot of my walking in the rain. There is something intensely refreshing about it. The rain inspires me, the rain clears my head. I have been known to announce that I am going for a walk, to be told that it is raining and reply that the rain is the reason why I am going for the walk.

The rain is the reason I took myself for a walk in St George's Park in Wandsworth a couple of years ago. The rain was the reason that there were puddles in the park. The rain was the reason that I found myself mesmerised by the drops of rain in the puddle. I found myself watching the drops and ripples and lost myself in another world. This experience inspired me to paint and I have been painting ever since. I may feel guided to share more in a later publication. We shall see.

Back to Wandsworth Common, a couple came towards me on the other side of the wide vehicle gravel path with a cute frisky little black terrier spaniel type dog. He walked beside them then scurried to the left of them before scurrying to the right of them, investigating a leaf here and a tree trunk there. When he spotted me he bounded straight over to me. He was adorable and seeing him advance towards me at speed was adorable too.

"Ooh, you're beautiful aren't you, have you come to say hallo?" I bent down and he offered me a paw. His people hurried over to stop him and apologised for his muddy paws on my clothes. He was really too cute for me to mind and I was simply delighted by his attention. The man said,

"Oh, he really likes you." Well, that was certainly nice to hear because I liked him too. I was even more flattered when the lady told me that their dog does not normally go to strangers. There I was again being told that same thing. Interesting.

*

Then there was the time I walked along the pavement towards a public house on the corner of a main road and side street. There were two men chatting outside, one had a dog on his leash tied around a lamppost, the other dog's lead was attached to the leg of a table. While the men conversed, the dogs had their own conversation, with a great deal of snapping, snarling, barking and baring of teeth they took it in turns or simultaneously raised their front legs and lunged towards each other. Their activity blocked the pathway, so it was understandable that people stepped off the pavement and walked into the road to get by. These dogs dominated the pavement and they had control.

I was getting closer. I could have crossed the road. I could have stepped off the kerb. My intention was not to worry about them. I just saw their behaviour as dogs doing what dogs do, I suppose. I expected all to be well. I continued to walk towards them. Just in time, the barking stopped, they retreated, legs down, no snapping, no snarling, no visible canine canines. I walked past, said thank you and was amused to hear the barking recommence moments later. So they were just playing after all. I have no explanation for it, perhaps there is nothing to explain. Who knows?

*

Then there was the time I walked from Covent Garden tube station towards Neal's Yard when I saw a Big Issue seller on the pavement ahead of me. On the ground beside him sat a ginger cat. Wait a minute I thought we were talking about dogs? Well that is exactly why I mention him because this cat seemed to behave like a dog. He sat on the pavement of a busy street and did not appear to mind the fast flow of pedestrian traffic rushing past them both. As I walked towards them I watched the man bend down and wrap a scarf around the cat's neck. Yes, he wrapped a scarf around the cat's neck. More to the point, the cat let him. I had never seen that before and I was fascinated because the cat just sat there and let the scarf be wrapped around him.

What also captured my attention was the way the guy behaved with the cat, it was a pure demonstration of love and affection and I felt like I was witnessing a powerful relationship, a friendship of trust and adoration. Yes, I did think all of that at the time. I remember feeling quite moved by the sight of them together.

Seeing them reminded me of the time I watched a woman with her dog on a bus. Her behaviour towards him and his response towards her made me think for the first time "Ah, so that must be what love is." It was a light bulb moment for me and bearing in mind that it was only about five years ago, this may give you some indication of the work which has been done. Coming from a place of not knowing or not remembering, I know now that I have achieved a vast amount by being able to recognise that love even exists.

The scarf was wrapped and gently tucked in, the man stood up and I smiled at him as I passed. I was still fascinated by the sight of a cat just sitting, just chillin' on the busy pavement but I did not want a magazine so I walked on. I could not get my mind off them, so turned and just watched them for a little longer. The man had a wonderful warm, soft energy about him and that had to be confirmed by the fact that he had a cat that was content to sit beside him anywhere, never mind there in such an environment. Cats are known for their propensity to please themselves, wander here, self-amuse, wander there, self-entertain, chill here, snooze there, not seeming to care about anyone or anything else. This cat was behaving like a dog, sitting with loyalty beside his lord and master or indeed, his best friend.

I still did not want a magazine but I followed my inspiration to walk back to the man with some money. He was already glowing and his lovely smile lit up his face when he saw me and said,

"Hallo lovely lady." Well, that was jolly nice of him. I said,

"Hi, I don't want a magazine but I'd like to give you some money for you to buy food for gorgeous cat."

"Oh thank you, that is kind of you, would you like to meet him, his name is Bob, he's Bob Cat." Then he looked down at his friend and said, "Say hallo to the beautiful lady, Bob." Well this was a couple of years ago but I remember it, like it was yesterday, the cat still curled up on the pavement, looked up from his comfortable neck wrapped position, gazed at me with a knowing expression then after what seemed like ages, looked away. Well, if I was fascinated before, I was even more fascinated after that. What kind of cat does that? This cat thought it was a dog.

I enjoyed a lovely conversation with the guy who told me about how he rescued Bob when he was a few months old and they have been inseparable ever since. I loved hearing about the way Bob sits on the chap's shoulders and across the back of his neck as they travel around, I think it would have been fun to see that. I left them and their unusual partnership, feeling that I had witnessed something truly special and it was an honour to have been in the right place at the right time. I felt blessed.

*

I have many random interactions with strangers so this book gives me an opportunity to share some that may seem stranger than strange. I am accustomed to it now. Occasionally when I share, someone might say that the event was a once in a lifetime experience, however, I know different.

One that springs to mind took place in a lovely restaurant where I was enjoying a lively lunch with a dear friend of mine. She is always fantastic fun to meet up with and a pleasure to be with. An hour with her feels like a year and five hours feels like five minutes. We were laughing our way through food and drink and I showed her my new crystal. In my right hand was a beautiful new wand of selenite which had recently been added to my collection, when a lady at another table called out,

"Do you put a pink one in the left hand?" I turned to see someone looking at me and smiling, yes she was talking to me. She asked again and as I happened to have one with me at the time, I picked up my rose quartz wand in my left hand and showed it to her. She laughed, her friend laughed and we laughed. How wonderful that she felt so comfortable and confident to call out to random people at other tables in restaurants. She asked if I did reiki because she had 'just guessed'. How cool is that? She turned out to be an alternative therapist like myself, so had similar interests. She amused me a little later by saying,

Carole Chandler

"I hope you didn't mind me interrupting you but my subconscious spoke to your subconscious and your subconscious told my subconscious that it would be alright to speak to you." Well, there was only one answer to that,

"Your subconscious was absolutely right."

Oh I do meet some interesting people.

*

Then there was the lovely sunny weekday morning when I had left home to walk to my therapy room ready for another day of energy balancing healing by reiki and massage. I had already meditated before breakfast as this continues to be my chosen way to begin the day. I have often invented ways of increasing my ability to focus and live life in the moment, increase my awareness and be present. There are many ways I do this and the conscious decision that I made to stop reading newspapers, stop listening to the news and concentrate on the beauty of my now has really helped. Another major factor which has really helped is that I no longer carry my mobile phone. I fully appreciate that this is not a solution for everyone for a variety of reasons. It seriously impacted on my ability to focus, to be present, to be aware and to be me. All of that waiting for it to ring, anticipated messages, unanswered texts, misunderstandings, frustrations, disappointments and negativity. One day I made the inspired decision to just live without it. I do still own one, an ancient one which I occasionally use for the calculator or alarm functions, however I can go for six weeks without turning it on. For me the difference has been significant, the impact enormous.

Anyway, I have no idea why I felt the impulse to say all of that, so let us return to the weekday morning in question when I had decided to employ one of my invented focus games. Sometimes during my walk I choose a colour, it can be any colour and I look out for it and have fun spotting it along my way. Anyway, it helps keeps me present, to focus, to stop worrying about the future or fuss about the past. I have been taught and now understand that they are both fruitless activities so to remain in my now is my goal. I frequently enjoy the evidence of this attitude, the benefits reveal themselves and for me, there is no escaping the importance of my now.

So on this morning I chose the colour pink. I was not concerned about the significance of choosing that particular colour on that particular day. I had the urge to go for pink so I followed it. Not just any pink, oh no, I was feeling specific. It was bright pink, it was fuchsia pink, a beautiful vibrant full on, in your face, powerful pink. I set off and spotted a bright pink sweet wrapper sitting by the kerb at the side of the road. It may have been considered as rubbish but it looked beautiful laying there in contrast to the dark grey kerb stones, grey pavement and black tarmacadam of the road. It made me smile.

A little further along my way, I saw a child's bicycle propped against a fence. It had a bright pink frame, with pink wheels, pink tassels hanging from the pink handle bars and a pink basket on the front. It made me smile.

A little further, I saw a pink sock, bright pink sock just lying there on the grass, a fuchsia pink sock all by itself. It made me smile.

A little further, I spotted a window with the white curtains still drawn. Between the curtains and the window pane was a piece of paper, a piece of pink paper about A4 size just hanging from the rail. It made me smile.

A little further, I noticed a woman way down the road on the other side. I passed a few shops on my way towards her and there were several people between us, all moving to and fro as normal for that time of day. She had caught my eye because of her skirt, her beautiful, vibrant, fuchsia pink skirt which was easily visible from a distance. She crossed the road and walked towards me. The pink skirted lady continued walking, she passed other people and instead of walking past me she stood in front of me, she stopped and I stopped. She smiled and handed me a piece of paper. I was feeling good, I had no concerns, I accepted the piece of paper and without looking at it, I thanked her and said,

"I was actually distracted by your beautiful skirt, what a gorgeous shade of pink."

"Oh thank you, this is the first time I've worn it. I usually wear black trousers and boots, I don't know why but today I felt like wearing a skirt and sandals." Interesting. Even though I have many unexplained encounters, I was intrigued by this.

"Your skirt is so beautiful that I noticed it from way down the road there." We exchanged pleasantries about the beauty of the day, wished each other well and parted. After a few paces I remembered the piece of paper, I stopped to check it out and found it was a printed sheet with a picture. I unfolded it and in big letters it read, 'the suffering will end soon'. Interesting. I smiled. I understood. I was at that time daily visiting a terminally ill relative in hospital. The message was timely. It brought comfort. The suffering did end soon. I felt no need to keep the paper the day she gave it to me, so I left it somewhere for someone else to find at a time that it may be needed. I thanked the Universe for the acknowledgement.

As the reader, I leave you to come to your own conclusions about who she was and why she wore a pink skirt and... and... and ... All I know is that once again I felt blessed.

*

Anyone would be forgiven for thinking that it was a random meeting indeed. Well what about the time I went for an evening walk in Putney. I started to walk across the bridge and stopped about a third of the way, with the distinct impulse that I should not go any further. I have learned to follow my inner guidance so I did not question myself. I retraced my steps a few paces and stood by the wall. I had no idea why I was standing there but it felt like the right thing to do at the time. It was a lovely evening in August and the setting sun was working some magic in the sky, treating me to pinks, blues, lilacs and yellows over the River Thames. I ignored the many people who walked past, as I simply enjoyed the beauty of the scene before me.

A man wheeled his bicycle past me, turned and stopped. I looked at him because he had stopped and to my amusement, found he was looking straight at me, so I smiled. He said,

"You're beautiful." Well that was nice of him to say so. He continued, "Wow, you really are beautiful." He turned himself and his bike and repositioned himself to stand in front of me. Yes you have guessed it, he blocked my view of the pastel river scene but never mind, he was not to know that. I thanked him for the compliment and he seemed happy enough to just continue looking at me, wearing some fancy multi glazed, triple lensed, bike shades, so I laughed and said I was surprised he could see me at all with those glasses on. I expected him to take them off but he said,

"Oh I don't just see you through my eyes, I see you through my body and through here", as he pointed above his head towards the vents of this crash helmet. Okay, I thought to myself, this is going to be interesting. He asked me if I knew what he meant and I said yes. He asked me if I was sure and I said yes. When he asked me what I do, I thought about it for a moment as my response varies depending on who is doing the asking. For him I went with,

"I balance energy and help people reduce their resistance to allow them to align with their inner being." He seemed comfortable with that. He asked me how, so I said that my work involves reiki and massage. Before answering the 'what is reiki' question, I thought about it for a moment as my response varies depending on who is doing the asking. For him I went with,

"It's Universal life force healing, I allow myself to be open and used for energy to flow through me for the benefit of the receiver." He seemed comfortable with that and asked,

"So you believe in higher forces then?" My answer was simple,

"I believe because I know about higher forces." By this point he was grinning across his face, he said,

"You'll never guess what I asked for today?" Well, that is not a game I usually feel inclined to join in with, so I smiled and waited for him to tell me if he wanted to.

"I asked the Universe to send me a woman, a real woman, a beautiful connected woman who understands how the spiritual world works. I asked for her and here you are." Er, okay, I had an idea this might be interesting.

We talked and talked, I could not see his eyes because he continued to wear his unusual bike glasses even as the twilight turned to night but he faced me the whole time seemingly very attentive. He had a lot of opinions and a lot to say, he asked questions, so many questions, some of which I felt happy to answer and some less so. He mentioned angels by name and I was interested when he mentioned the name of one of my spiritual guides. He had a lot to say about names, particularly his own and he told me about how children stop him in the street, a little like the experiences I have. At one point he randomly asked me if I can sing. We talked for so long that the sun had gone completely and the beautiful pastel sky had been seamlessly replaced by an equally beautiful indigo. He did not seem bothered by the drop in temperature even though his strong muscular slim frame only wore a sleeveless top and bike shorts. I was pleased to be wearing a sweater and thick jacket and was glad that I had my scarf with me. Interestingly, he kept his heavily tinted bike glasses on even when it was dark, so throughout our encounter I never saw his eyes.

He asked me which way I was going and I said that I was happy just where I was, that I had been enjoying the sunset when he arrived and he apologised for interrupting (although there was no need). For the first time in our conversation he seemed distracted for a moment, he rummaged in his bag, took out a piece of paper, rummaged some more then put the paper back. He announced he was leaving and assured me that Universal forces would ensure that we meet again. He then walked back in the same direction from which he had arrived.

Oh, I do meet some interesting people.

*

Once again, anyone would be forgiven for thinking that it was a random meeting indeed. Well what about the time when I was browsing in one of my favourite shops in Covent Garden. I love being surrounded by the music and smells and they fill the shop with spiritual paraphernalia to suit anyone wherever they may be on their spiritual journey. I had settled in the book section all alone looking at a little A6 size book which I had found lying on its side on the top shelf.

It held my attention for a while and I was in no hurry just enjoying my time on my own. I flicked through the pages until I stopped at a page that seemed to grip me. I had no idea why, I just knew that I liked what I saw. It was a drawing of a collection of circles arranged in a specific configuration of hexagons, triangles and rectangles, with lines added at regular angles. It looked spectacular and I stared at the page in an effort to absorb the image.

I knew that I was on my own and had the doorways in view, so imagine my surprise when I heard a voice say,

"That's interesting." I looked up to see a tall handsome man with a warm happy face, an engaging smile and gorgeous, bright, dark brown eyes. He was a vision of beauty. I looked up into those fine eyes and smiled, wondering silently to myself where he could possibly have come from. He continued,

"That's interesting, is it sacred geometry?" Without words, I turned to the cover of the book to show him the title and it was called exactly that, 'Sacred Geometry'. I did not have time to wonder what to make of that because once more he said, "That's interesting," then reached behind him, put his hand into a pocket, retrieved a rolled up sheet of white A4 paper, unfurled it and held it open for me to see. On it was the exact same image which I had been mesmerised by in the little book. He showed me the same number of circles, the same configuration of hexagons, triangles and rectangles and lines. Well it was my turn to say 'interesting', for want of a more appropriate word, which I had no access to in the moment as I was pretty gobsmacked.

He was a sheer delight and told me that he carries the image around with him to consecrate his food. How? He puts the paper on the table, the plate on the paper to bless the food before consuming. Well this was certainly unusual for me to hear and I liked the idea of it.

We chatted for ages, easily and comfortably. He was a joy to meet and a special person to share ideas with. He complimented me, my eyes, my face, my smile, my clothes, my energy and my aura. He had a lot to say about my aura. He said so many lovely things about me and it was really nice to hear them. He told me about his family, his childhood, his work, his goals and his aspirations. This lovely man asked questions, lots of questions and showed interest in my thoughts about life, the universe and everything. He seemed to enjoy my perspective and thanked me for my view, clarity and explanations. It was so kind of him to say that he found me inspiring. In response to his enquiry about the specific teachings that I follow, I showed him a copy of *'Ask and It Is Given'* lovingly brought to us by Esther and Jerry Hicks, which was on the shelf in front of us. It clearly defines the *Universal Law of Attraction* and I told him that the book explains absolutely everything.

It was at that moment that I felt the inspiration to wish him well and depart. I really enjoyed meeting him and our interaction was clearly a special moment but I felt that it was time to move on. I love the shop and was in there regularly about the same time the same day of the week for more than year after our meeting and I never saw him again.

Oh, I do meet some interesting people.

As it happens the circle grid that connected us on that morning has since been the basis of a lot of my meditation inspired art, which keeps me joyfully occupied when I am not writing or dancing or walking or cycling or travelling on buses. I have reproduced the grid many times and have a variety of versions adorning the walls of my home. Ooh, now I have a strong urge to write a book about my art and meditation, perhaps that is a project for the future. We shall see.

*

My life if good, I acknowledge it, I am grateful for it. Now that I understand how the world works, I do not give anyone else the responsibility of creating my happiness. There is so much freedom in knowing that my joy is down to me. I know it and I feel it and I guess it shows. I know that people see it because they tell me. Brace yourself, here are a few of those people...

There was the time when a work colleague unexpectedly asked me a question one day,

"You are always reading something and I want to know what it is because every time I look at you, I see a smile on your face. I want some of that." I was reading a book that I have dipped into regularly since I discovered it or it discovered me several years ago and changed my life. Yes, it was the same book which I showed to the lovely guy of the sacred geometry interaction. The book makes me smile because it gives me understanding, it explains who, what, why, where, when and how. It has the power to make anyone smile.

Then there was the Monday morning at breakfast on the last day of my jive holiday in Devon's seaside resort of Torquay. I had not met any of them before the weekend began. There were eight of us enjoying easy flowing conversation when from the other end of the table a lady shouted across,

"Carole, I want to know how it is that you are so positive all of the time. I want some to that." She surprised me with her outburst because we had spoken to each other very little during the weekend and I had no recollection of doing or saying anything out of the ordinary for her to have that impression of me. My guidance was to respond by saying something about knowing what I want and knowing how to ask for it and interestingly this led to much discussion.

Then there was the time I walked across London's ever busy Leicester Square when a charity collector stopped me, insisting that he could tell that I would be happy to spend a moment talking to him. I did not need to think long about it, I had a moment to spare and his warm face, big smile and joyous disposition seemed good enough reasons to give him a moment of my time. He asked me if I supported his charity. I told him I support everyone. He fired lovely compliments at me one after the other, about how he thought I was this and that and about how happy he was to meet me. No matter what I said he seemed bowled over by it. Then even I was surprised when he said,

"You're amazing, can I give you a hug?" It seemed like a sensible idea to confirm,

"You want to give me a hug?"

"Yes please, do you mind if I give you a hug?" I could see no reason to decline his kind offer, so when he raised and extended his arms out far from his side, I raised and extended my own. We hugged right there in the street. It was quite a moment, he was a lovely young man and I felt honoured to be viewed in such a positive light by a total stranger. He did not even ask for money for his charity and exchanging good wishes I started to walk away when he shouted after me,

"You're an angel you are." How sweet.

Then there was the Friday morning I walked along the river Thames just about to pass Lambeth House, when I saw a couple of Kevlar clad police officers deep in conversation leaning against a wall. Imagine my amusement as I walked closer, when one of them stepped forward simply to tell me that he liked my beautiful smile. Really! He was in uniform and yet he felt so inspired to compliment me. Wow.

Then there was the time, on another Friday, I was walking along Drury Lane, a woman stopped in front of me to tell me that I looked happy and peaceful. This was particularly welcome as I was walking in the rain without an umbrella.

Then there was the time I was in a shop in Streatham, when the owner said he liked my smile and asked me which religion I belong to. I confidently told him that I do not follow any particular religion and that I embrace all faiths. He said that he could see that I may not be religious but I was spiritual and said,

"You don't just look happy, you look peaceful too." Oh bless him.

Then there was the time when a green van stopped to let me cross the zebra crossing on Garratt Lane in Wandsworth. It was a brilliant sunny day and the sunshine bounced off the windscreen, which meant that I could not see inside the vehicle. I waved, smiled and said thank you anyway. Before I reached the other side of the road, the front seat passenger leaned out of the window and shouted at me,

"I like your smile." Ooh er, that was nice. I carried on walking and as the van went past me again, I heard the driver toot his horn, I looked across to see them both frantically waving at me. Bless them both, how sweet.

Then there was the time when I walked past a bus stop on my way to Tooting Broadway and a guy leapt out from the bus shelter to tell me that he liked my smile. How nice.

Another time I walked past Wimbledon train station and a chap weaved through a crowd of people to stand in front of me and tell me that I am beautiful. How lovely.

Then there was the time when I waited for a bus on Garratt Lane, a chap stopped to stare at me, "Wow, you are beautiful," he paused, I thanked him, he carried on staring, "I swear to god you really are." He just continued to stare until I broke his trance by thanking him again, giving him permission to enjoy the rest of his day and move on. It was certainly very nice of him to tell me what he thought, as there is nothing quite like being praised and being positively held by someone as their object of attention.

Then there was the time I waited for a friend outside the ladies' loo, during the interval of a wonderful night out to see 'Dreamboats and Petticoats' in a London theatre. A couple of women loudly discussed their desire and urgent need for a faster moving queue. One of them pointed at me and said,

"Look at her over there looking all glamorous, I'll bet she never needs to cross her legs and hope she doesn't wet her knickers." I chose to believe that they were attempting to compliment me and they freely admitted that their northern English humour is sometimes misunderstood down here in the south. She said again that she thought I looked glamorous and I thanked her.

Then there was the time when a friendly postman introduced himself to me in Wimbledon as I walked the short cut behind a pub on my way to work. He was just the loveliest man with a gorgeous smile and a bubbly personality. He shook my hand and said that he had seen me around and was hoping for an opportunity to meet me. Wow, what a delightful thing for a stranger to say.

Then there was the time when my meal was served by a delightful lady in a wonderful restaurant which I visit frequently. I showed my appreciation by saying, "Thank you very much, you're an angel," to which she replied, "From one to another." How cool is that? Often people deny any reference to their divinity because they do not see it or feel it. To my joy, she not only accepted it but offered a reflection in response. I was touched.

Then there was the guy who worked in the reception of a hotel, where I stayed for a few days. Everyone was friendly but this particular chap smiled broadly, waved enthusiastically and said hallo joyfully every time I walked past, regardless of what he was doing. On one occasion I thanked him for always greeting me so warmly and he said,

"It's you, there is something about you, I can't help it, you just make me smile every time I see you." Oh bless him, what an absolutely lovely thing for him to say.

Then there was the time I passed a group of people leaning against the railings outside Tooting Broadway underground station, when one of the guys stepped away from the others to stand in front of me and tell me that he liked my smile. Oh, how lovely.

Then there was the time I heard glorious music as I walked past a stall at a Mind Body Spirit festival, in London. The angelic voice that I could hear belonged to the beautiful lady standing behind the table and the delicious musical accompaniment was exquisitely performed by her husband. I bought a CD and she gave me another as a free gift, signed it for me and we hugged with a warm I-feel-like-I-have-known-you-forever kind of hug.

Then there was the time when I stayed at a hotel for a few days, when the chef came to my table during breakfast to say hallo and enjoy a friendly chat. He introduced himself, shook my hand asked my name, showed interest in what I do for a living and told me that he had noticed me when I first arrived and liked the way I looked happy and peaceful.

Then there was the guy selling macaroons from a stall at the South Bank weekend world food market. His smiley face and friendly disposition already had my attention when he asked if I had been enjoying my day. I felt inspired to tell him that I was writing a book and I particularly enjoyed writing in the atmosphere of the Royal Festival Hall. He asked questions, showed interest so I told him the book was about me and my life and my experiences. He encouraged me with his few words,

"I think it's great that you are writing about yourself, I like real stories about real people, I'm sure it will be a good book." How sweet of the Macaroon Man to be so supportive.

Then there were the guys stopping passers-by in Covent Garden. One pointed at me and said to the other,

"Ask her, she's got it going on." I am led to understand by my children that this is a compliment. As it turned out, he was offering makeovers, glamming sessions, before and after photographic packages. No, he was not saying that I needed improvement and yes, he agreed that I already looked beautiful. Realising that I was not fitting in with his script, he seemed unsure of how to proceed. I basically told him that he was asking the wrong person. His offer was not desirable to me as I could not look or feel better than I did right then and there at that moment in time. He put his hand on my arm and said that he wished more women were like me.

Then there was the guy who gave me two extra stamps on my loyalty card in a coffee shop in Holborn just because he liked my smile.

Then there was the young lady who gave me extra stamps on my restaurant loyalty card in Wimbledon for no apparent reason. How lovely.

Then there was the guy who gave me extra stamps on my loyalty card in a café in Battersea again for the fun of it I guess. How nice.

Then there was the lady in the fancy restaurant in Covent Garden who disappeared into the kitchen when I asked her about a cheese listed on the menu. I had not heard of it before, so when she returned with a packet, I assumed she was showing me the label for information. I thanked her and was grateful that she went to so much trouble to answer my question, then she gave me the packet. I mean really, how sweet is that?

Then there was the time I had a laugh and a joke with a couple of cashiers in a TKMaxx in London. We were all in a good mood and I had fun with them while I paid for my three items. My cashier announced that she was a manager and had decided to take advantage of her authority by giving me a thirty per cent discount purely because she liked me. What a hoot.

Then there was the time I travelled north of Watford to see my favourite musical. After telling me that the same day performance was practically sold out, the lovely chap at the box office, found me one of the best seats in the house and just because he liked me, sold me the ticket at fifty per cent off. Ooh, life is sweet.

Then there was the guy who jumped in front of me at the Winter Wonderland Christmas extravaganza in London's Hyde Park. A propos of nothing, he appeared before me, grinned and waved a teddy bear in front of my face shouting, "Everybody loves you."

*

What can I say? This is me, this is my life, at least it is a glimpse anyway. I appreciate that this book will not appeal to everyone. Of course not, how could it? I understand that some people may not get it but then again some people do not get me. That is okay too. A girl at work once described me as, *'always happy, a little bit high sometimes but always happy'*. There was not much I could say to that and I did not feel inclined to disagree with her either.

I also make no apology for my frequent use of the words amazing, beautiful, delightful, fantastic, gorgeous, lovely, radiant, warm and wonderful. They describe how I see the world about me and are just a representation of my perspective of life.

My dearest son despairs with me sometimes and made me laugh once when after one of my 'everything is okay' responses he said,

"Oh what's the point, you're like a Disney character you are." For some reason I really like that.

I offer these words merely as an option, a suggestion, perhaps an alternative. The experiences I have now would have seemed impossible to me from my previous emotional viewpoint. Perhaps they were impossible. Perhaps I did not have access to them.

How do we know what to aim for unless we can dream of it?

I dreamed of a life where people were nice to me. Here I am.

To the readers who have given up with my sharings, I wish them well. If you are still reading, then my words probably resonate with you on some level. If you have already discovered the *Law of Attraction*, congratulations, however, if you have not yet made it a conscious part of your life, then perhaps you feel inspired to take a look at some truly life changing material.

My tales are a far from exhaustive account, each and every day brings new joy, so many people have been met, so many words have been spoken, so many events have occurred, simply too many to write them all. See this as a taster. My experiences are a glimpse of possibilities, yes, that is it, a glimpse of possibilities.

I could write this book forever because my interactions are a joyful continuation, different days, different places and different people. With that in mind, I have to stop some time, so this feels like an appropriate place to draw these words to a close. I am bursting with excitement about sharing my numerous bus related encounters so after a well-earned rest, I intend to make that my next project.

Thank you to my wonderful children, who continue to teach and inspire me every moment of every day. Bless you both.

Thank you to the Wholemeal Café angels, for creating a divine space and keeping me fed and watered during my many hours of writing. Bless you all.

Thank you to everyone I have ever met no matter how brief the interaction. Without all of you I would not be the person I am today and these books would not exist.

Just for fun, you will find information about my energy balancing treatments on www.massageforinnerpeace.co.uk where I have also have listed some of the books and music which have contributed to my journey. However top of my reading list is *'Ask And It Is Given – The Teachings of Abraham',* Esther and Jerry Hicks as well as *'Illusions – The Adventures of a Reluctant Messiah',* Richard Bach. Top of my listening list is anything by *Sacred Earth Music,* Prem and Joshua Williams.

If you fancy a little further browsing, you will find examples of my meditation inspired art on www.celestialcircles.co.uk

A wise person once said, *'if you always do what you've always done, you'll always get what you always got'*.

I wish you everything I wish for myself, joy, love and peace.

Carole